Apr. 2013

SCHOLASTIC

FEBRUARY
Monthly Idea Book

Ready-to-Use Templates, Activities, Management Tools, and More — for Every Day of the Month

Karen Sevaly

New York • Toronto • London • Auckland • Sydney
Mexico City • New Delhi • Hong Kong • Buenos Aires

Teaching Resources

DEDICATION

This book is dedicated to teachers and children everywhere.

Cover design by Maria Lilja
Cover art by Jillian Phillips
Interior design by Melinda Belter
Illustrations by Maxie Chambliss, Sue Dennen, and Karen Sevaly

ISBN 978-0-545-37938-0

1 2 3 4 5 6 7 8 9 10   40   19 18 17 16 15 14 13

CONTENTS

FAVORITE TOPICS

GROUNDHOG DAY!

CONTENTS

VALENTINE'S DAY

Reproducible Patterns

HEART HEALTH

PRESIDENTS' DAY

AFRICAN AMERICAN ACHIEVEMENT

Reproducible Patterns

DENTAL HEALTH

AWARDS, INCENTIVES, AND MORE

ANSWER KEY

INTRODUCTION

Welcome to the original Monthly Idea Book series! This book was written especially for teachers getting ready to teach topics related to the month of February.

Each book in this month-by-month series is filled with dozens of ideas for PreK–3 classrooms. Activities connect to the Common Core State Standards for Reading (Foundational Skills), among other subjects, to help you meet the needs of your students. (For more information, see page 16.)

Most everything you need to prepare the lessons and activities in this resource is included, such as:

- calendar and weather-related props

- book cover patterns and stationery for writing assignments

- booklet patterns

- games and puzzles that support learning in curriculum areas such as math, science, and writing

- activity sheets that help students organize information, respond to learning, and explore topics in a meaningful way

- patterns for projects that connect to holidays, special occasions, and commemorative events

All year long, you can weave the ideas and reproducible patterns in these unique books into your monthly lesson plans and classroom activities. Happy teaching!

What's Inside

You'll find that this book is chock-full of reproducibles that make lesson planning easier:

- puppets and picture props

- bookmarks, booklets, and book covers

- game boards, puzzles, and word finds

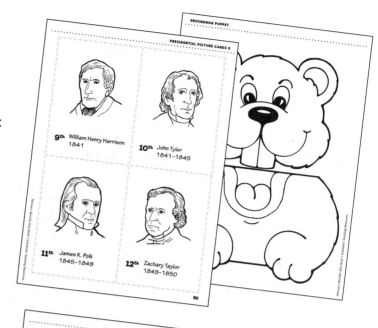

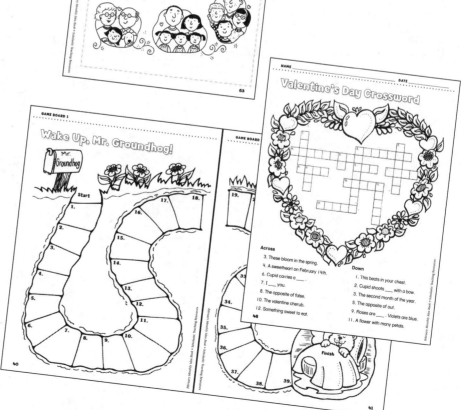

■ stationery

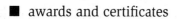

■ awards and certificates

How to Use This Book

The reproducible pages in this book have flexible use and may be modified to meet your particular classroom needs. Use the reproducible activity pages and patterns in conjunction with the suggested activities or weave them into your curriculum in other ways.

★ PHOTOCOPY OR SCAN

To get started, think about your developing lesson plans and upcoming bulletin boards. If desired, carefully remove the pages you will need. Duplicate those pages on copy paper, color paper, tagboard, or overhead transparency sheets. If you have access to a scanner, consider saving the pattern pages as PDF files. That way, you can size images up or down and customize them with text to create individualized lessons, center-time activities, interactive whiteboard lessons, homework pages, and more.

★ LAMINATE FOR DURABILITY

Laminating the reproducibles will help you extend their use. If you have access to a roll laminator, then you already know how fortunate you are when it comes to saving time and resources. If you don't have a laminator, clear adhesive vinyl covering works well. Just sandwich the pattern between two sheets of vinyl and cut off any excess. Then try some of these ideas:

- Put laminated sheets of stationery in a writing center to use for handwriting practice. Wipe-off markers work great on coated pages and can easily be erased with dry tissue.

- Add longevity to calendars, weather-related pictures, and pocket chart rebus pictures by preserving them with lamination.

- Transform picture props into flannel board figures. After lamination, add a tab of hook-and-loop fastener to the back of the props and invite students to adhere them to the flannel board for storytelling fun.

- To enliven magnet board activities, affix sections of magnet tape to the back of the picture props. Then encourage students to sort images according to the skills you're working on. For example, you might have them group images by commonalities such as initial sound, habitat, or physical attributes.

★ BULLETIN BOARDS

1. Set the Stage

Use background paper colors that complement many themes and seasons. For example, the dark background you used as a spooky display in October will have dramatic effect in November, when you begin a unit on woodland animals or Thanksgiving.

While paper works well, there are other background options available. You might also try fabric from a colorful bed sheet or gingham material. Discontinued rolls of patterned wallpaper can be purchased at discount stores. What's more, newspapers are easy to use and readily available. Attach a background of comics to set off a lesson on riddles, or use grocery store flyers to provide food for thought on a bulletin board about nutrition.

2. Make the Display

The reproducible patterns in this book can be enlarged to fit your needs. When we say enlarge, we mean it! Think BIG! Use an overhead projector to enlarge the images you need to make your bulletin board extraordinary.

If your school has a stencil press, you're lucky. The rest of us can use these strategies for making headers and titles.

- Cut strips of paper, cloud shapes, or cartoon bubbles. They will all look great! Then, by hand, write the text using wide-tipped permanent markers or tempera paint.

- If you must cut individual letters, use 4- by 6-inch pieces of construction paper. (Laminate first, if you can.) Cut the uppercase letters as shown on page 14. No need to measure, as somewhat irregular letters will look creative, not messy.

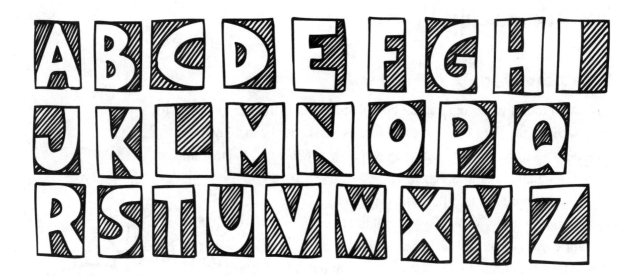

3. Add Color and Embellishments

Use your imagination! You'll be surprised at the great displays you can create.

- Watercolor markers work great on small areas. On larger areas, you can switch to crayons, color chalk, or pastels. (Lamination will keep the color off of you. No laminator? A little hairspray will do the trick as a fixative.)

- Cut character eyes and teeth from white paper and glue them in place. The features will really stand out and make your bulletin boards engaging.

- For special effects, include items that provide texture and visual interest, such as buttons, yarn, and lace. Try cellophane or blue glitter glue on water scenes. Consider using metallic wrapping paper or aluminum foil to add a bit of shimmer to stars and belt buckles.

- Finally, take a picture of your completed bulletin board. Store the photos in a recipe box or large sturdy envelope. Next year when you want to create the same display, you'll know right where everything goes. You might even want to supply students with pushpins and invite them to recreate the display, following your directions and using the photograph as support.

Staying Organized

Organizing materials with monthly file folders provides you with a location to save reproducible activity pages and patterns, along with related craft ideas, recipes, and magazine or periodical articles.

If you prefer, use file boxes instead of folders. You'll find that with boxes there will plenty of room to store enlarged patterns, sample art projects, bulletin board materials, and much more.

Meeting the Standards

CONNECTIONS TO THE COMMON CORE STATE STANDARDS

The Common Core State Standards Initiative (CCSSI) has outlined learning expectations in English/Language Arts, among other subject areas, for students at different grade levels. In general, the activities in this book align with the following standards for students in grades K–3. For more information, visit the CCSSI website at www.corestandards.org.

Reading: Foundational Skills

Print Concepts
- RF.K.1, RF.1.1. Demonstrate understanding of the organization and basic features of print.

Phonics and Word Recognition
- RF.K.3, RF.1.3, RF.2.3, RF.3.3. Know and apply grade-level phonics and word analysis skills in decoding words.

Fluency
- RF.K.4. Read emergent-reader texts with purpose and understanding.
- RF.1.4, RF.2.4, RF.3.4. Read with sufficient accuracy and fluency to support comprehension.

Writing

Production and Distribution of Writing
- W.3.4. Produce writing in which the development and organization are appropriate to task and purpose.
- W.K.5, W.1.5, W.2.5, W.3.5. Focus on a topic and strengthen writing as needed by revising and editing.

Research to Build and Present Knowledge
- W.K.7, W.1.7, W.2.7. Participate in shared research and writing projects.
- W.3.7. Conduct short research projects that build knowledge about a topic.
- W.K.8, W.1.8, W.2.8, W.3.8. Recall information from experiences or gather information from provided sources to answer a question.

Range of Writing
- W.3.10. Write routinely over extended time frames (time for research, reflection, and revision) and shorter time frames (a single sitting or a day or two) for a range of discipline-specific tasks, purposes, and audiences.

Speaking & Listening

Comprehension and Collaboration
- SL.K.1, SL.1.1, SL.2.1. Participate in collaborative conversations with diverse partners about grade-level topics and texts with peers and adults in small and larger groups.
- SL.K.2, SL.1.2, SL.2.2, SL.3.2. Recount or describe key ideas or details from a text read aloud or information presented orally or through other media.
- SL.K.3, SL.1.3, SL.2.3, SL.3.3. Ask and answer questions about what a speaker says in order to gather additional information or clarify something that is not understood.

Presentation of Knowledge and Ideas
- SL.K.4, SL.1.4, SL.2.4. Describe people, places, things, and events with relevant details, expressing ideas and feelings clearly.
- SL.K.5, SL.1.5, SL.2.5, SL.3.5. Add drawings or other visual displays to stories or recounts of experiences when appropriate to clarify ideas, thoughts, and feelings.

Language

Conventions of Standard English
- L.K.1, L.1.1, L.2.1, L.3.1. Demonstrate command of the conventions of standard English grammar and usage when writing or speaking.
- L.K.2, L.1.2, L.2.2, L.3.2. Demonstrate command of the conventions of standard English capitalization, punctuation, and spelling when writing.

Knowledge of Language
- L.2.3, L.3.3. Use knowledge of language and its conventions when writing, speaking, reading, or listening.

Vocabulary Acquisition and Use
- L.K.4, L.1.4, L.2.4, L.3.4. Determine or clarify the meaning of unknown and multiple-meaning words and phrases based on grade level reading and content, choosing flexibly from an array of strategies.
- L.K.6, L.1.6, L.2.6, L.3.6. Use words and phrases acquired through conversations, reading and being read to, and responding to texts.

CALENDAR TIME

Getting Started

February

Sunday	Monday	Tuesday	Wednesday	Thursday	Friday	Saturday

19

CALENDAR

★ MARK YOUR CALENDAR

Make photocopies of the calendar grid on page 19 and use it to meet your needs. Consider using the write-on spaces to:

- write the corresponding numerals for each day

- mark and count how many days have passed

- track the weather with stamps or stickers

- note student birthdays

- record homework assignments

- communicate with families about positive behaviors

- remind volunteers about schedules, field trips, shortened days, and so on

CELEBRATIONS THIS MONTH

Whether you post a photocopy of pages 20 through 23 near your class calendar or just turn to these pages for inspiration, you're sure to find lots of information on them to discuss with students. To take celebrating and learning a step further, invite the class to add more to the list. For example, students can add anniversaries of significant events and the birthdays of their favorite authors or historical figures.

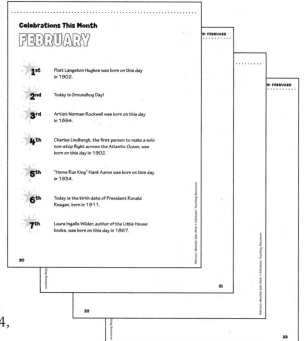

CALENDAR HEADER

You can make a photocopy of the header on page 24, color it, and use it as a title for your classroom calendar. You might opt to give the coloring job to a student who has a birthday that month. The student is sure to enjoy seeing his or her artwork each and every day of the month.

BEFORE INTRODUCING WHAT'S THE WEATHER?

Make a photocopy of the body template on page 25. Laminate it so you can use it again and again. Before sharing the template with the class, cut out pieces of cloth in the shapes of clothing students typically wear this month. For example, if you live in a warm weather climate, your February attire might include shorts and t-shirts. If you live in chillier climates, your attire might include a scarf, hat, and coat. Fit the cutouts to the body outline. When the clothing props are made, and you're ready to have students dress the template, display the clothing. Invite the "weather helper of the day" to tell what pieces of clothing he or she would choose to dress appropriately for the weather. (For extra fun, use foam to cut out accessories such as an umbrella, sunhat, and raincoat.

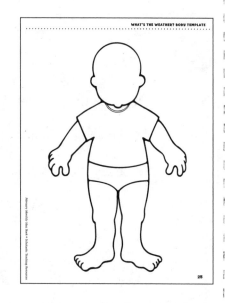

February

Sunday	Monday	Tuesday	Wednesday	Thursday	Friday	Saturday

Celebrations This Month

FEBRUARY

1st Poet Langston Hughes was born on this day in 1902.

2nd Today is Groundhog Day!

3rd Artist Norman Rockwell was born on this day in 1894.

4th Charles Lindbergh, the first person to make a solo non-stop flight across the Atlantic Ocean, was born on this day in 1902.

5th "Home Run King" Hank Aaron was born on this day in 1934.

6th Today is the birth date of President Ronald Reagan, born in 1911.

7th Laura Ingalls Wilder, author of the Little House books, was born on this day in 1867.

February Monthly Idea Book © Scholastic Teaching Resources

8th The Boy Scouts of America was founded on this day in 1910.

9th The United States government established the National Weather Service on this day in 1870.

10th American swimmer Mark Spitz, winner of nine Olympic gold medals, was born on this day in 1950.

11th American inventor Thomas Alva Edison was born on this day in 1847.

12th Abraham Lincoln, 16th president of the United States, was born on this day in 1809.

13th The last original "Peanuts" comic strip ran in newspapers on this day in 2000, one day after the death of its creator, Charles Schulz.

14th Today is St. Valentine's Day!

15th Today is the birth date of Susan B. Anthony, a women's rights advocate born in 1820.

16th The first 9-1-1 call was made in Haleyville, Alabama, on this day in 1968.

17th The National Parent Teacher Association (PTA) was established on this day in 1897.

18th On this day in 1930, astronomer Clyde W. Tombaugh discovered Pluto, which was identified as a planet at that time. In 2006, Pluto was recategorized as a dwarf planet.

19th Polish astronomer Nicolaus Copernicus was born on this day in 1473.

20th On this day in 1962, astronaut John Glenn became the first American to orbit the earth.

21st Today is the observance of International Mother Language Day, a day set aside to promote awareness of linguistic and cultural diversity.

22nd George Washington, the first president of the United States, was born on this day in 1732.

February Monthly Idea Book © Scholastic Teaching Resources

23rd German-English composer George Frederick Handel was born on this day in 1685.

24th Today is Mexican Flag Day, a national holiday in Mexico observed every year on this day since 1937.

25th *The Ranger*, the first United States aircraft carrier, was launched on this day in 1933.

26th Congress designated the Grand Canyon as a national park on this day in 1919.

27th Today is the birth date of poet Henry Wadsworth Longfellow, who was born in 1807.

28th The first televised basketball game was aired from Madison Square Garden on this day in 1940.

29th This date marks a leap year, a calendar event that occurs every four years.

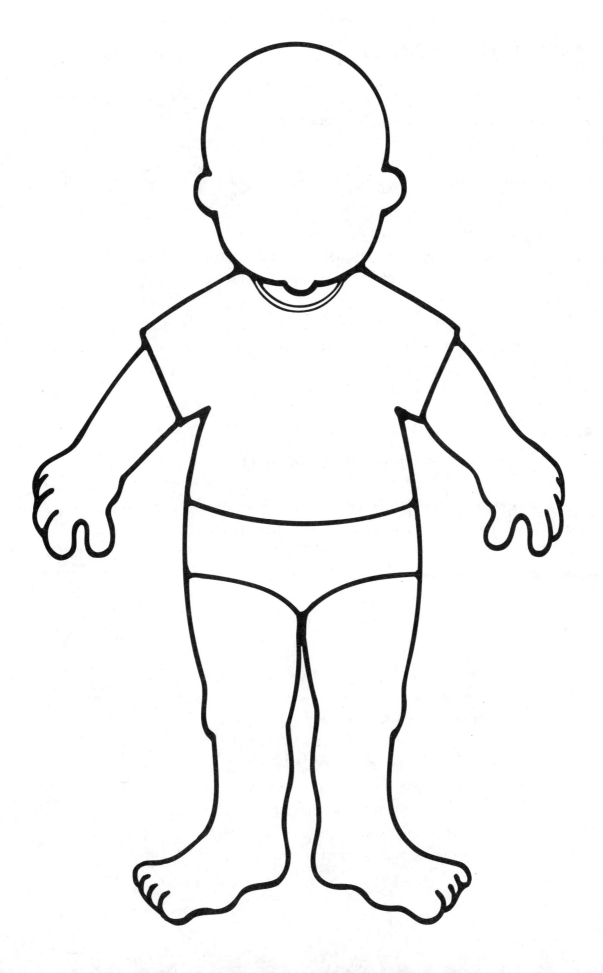

GROUNDHOG DAY!

The origin of Groundhog Day traces back to folk stories told in England and Germany. The date of February 2 was selected in honor of the Christian holiday of Candlemas.

The tradition of looking to a groundhog's behavior for a sign of spring grew out of observations of hibernating animals. It was believed that those animals would check the weather outside their dens and then decide whether to go back to sleep for the remainder of winter or stay awake for the early arrival of springtime.

The town of Punxsutawney in Pennsylvania gains its claim to fame from a groundhog named Punxsutawney Phil. Each year, tourists and reporters crowd around Phil's burrow on Gobbler's Knob to learn news of whether or not he sees his shadow and if there will be six more weeks of winter.

Leap Year

The Gregorian calendar is based upon the time it takes for the Earth to make one complete revolution around the Sun, which is 365 days, 5 hours and 48 minutes. The extra minutes eventually add up to an extra day. So, every four years we add it to the end of the month of February (Leap Year).

Suggested Activities

 ## ★ SIX MORE WEEKS?

On February 2, ask students to record the weather. Then ask: *Would the groundhog be able to see his shadow?* Take a vote and record the results on a class board, noting students' guesses about whether spring will come early or if there will be six more weeks of winter. Follow up by asking students to record the weather for the next six weeks. Make several photocopies of the chart (page 31) to help keep track of precipitation and temperatures. Invite volunteers to fill in the chart each day. At the end of the six weeks, discuss their findings. Was Punxsutawney Phil's prediction correct?

★ MEASURING SHADOWS

This activity is one you'll want to start early in the school day and continue throughout the day. First, distribute a photocopy of the record sheet on page 32 to each student. Explain that you will divide the class into small groups and then go outdoors. (Choose a sunny day for this activity.) There, students will use tape measures to find the length of their shadows and make observations about their findings. Throughout the day—perhaps hourly—have groups return to the same area and measure their shadows again. At the end of the day, invite volunteers from each group to share insights about why the length of their shadows varied at different times of the day. Finally, talk about what part of the day would be the best time to invite Punxsutawney Phil out of his burrow to look for his shadow.

★ PUNXSUTAWNEY PHIL POP-UP

According to Groundhog-Day tradition, Punxsutawney Phil comes out of his underground burrow on February 2 to "predict" the change of the season. If that day is sunny and Phil spots his shadow, he retreats into his burrow for at least six more weeks. This is viewed as an indicator that winter will last another six weeks. Cloudy skies on that day would prevent Phil from seeing his shadow. In this case, the forecast is that spring will arrive early.

Students can make pop-up puppets to help dramatize Phil's actions on Groundhog Day. Provide small groups with photocopies of the groundhog pattern (page 33), craft sticks, paper cups, green construction paper, and glue. To make a pop-up puppet, have each student do the following:

1. Color and cut out a groundhog pattern. Glue the cutout to a craft-stick handle.

2. Make a one-inch slit in the bottom of a cup.

3. Cut a 2-inch wide strip of green construction paper, making it long enough to fit around the cup rim.

4. Fringe one long edge of the paper strip. Glue the strip—fringe end up—around the rim of the cup, as shown.

5. From the inside of the cup, poke the puppet handle through the slit in the cup bottom.

6. Slide the handle up and down to make the groundhog come out of or go back into its cup burrow.

★ GROUNDHOG PAPER-BAG PUPPET

Send home with each student a photocopy of the groundhog puppet patterns (page 34) and a small paper bag. Explain that, as homework, students should find out surprising ways that people around the world predict weather and the change of seasons. They can interview family members, read books, and visit weather-related websites to learn interesting details about forecasting weather. After gathering their fun facts, students can make their puppets by gluing the groundhog head to the bottom of their paper bag and the body to the front of the bag. After assembling, they can use their puppet at home to practice telling what they have learned. Back at school, invite students to take turns performing with their puppets to share their findings with the class. (Most students will need a few days to complete this assignment.)

GROUNDHOG PUPPET

34

★ WEEKS-OF-WINTER STATIONERY

Invite students to learn more about Punxsutawney Phil at his website, www.groundhog.org, the Punxsutawney Groundhog Club. The site is helpful for lesson planning—for math and science activities, groundhog-inspired writing ideas, and more.

Afterward, ask students to create their own predictions about spring weather. Distribute photocopies of the stationery (page 35) to students on which to write. You might also invite students to write their predictions on e-cards delivered to your school e-mail account. This website offers dozens of Groundhog Day cards: www.punchbowl. com/ecards/groundhog-day.

WEEKS-OF-WINTER STATIONERY

35

★ HIBERNATION INVESTIGATION

Have students research hibernation to learn why some animals are true hibernators and others are not. Encourage them to use both school and local library resources to discover strategies that mammals, amphibians, reptiles, and other animals use to survive the harsh winter weather and scarcity of food. Students can use the stationery (page 35) to record their research and then bind their pages behind a copy of the Hibernation Investigation Book Cover (page 36). After assembling their report, invite students to write their name on the author line and color the cover.

★ GROUNDHOG DAY WORD FIND

Distribute copies of the word find on page 37 to reinforce what students have learned about Groundhog Day and the animal this special day is named for. After students complete the activity, have them use some of the words from the puzzle to write about a groundhog.

★ GROUNDHOG DAY CROSSWORD

Give students practice with Groundhog-Day vocabulary and developing problem-solving skills with the crossword puzzle on page 38. Distribute photocopies to students, then demonstrate how to use the clues to find the answers and fill in the puzzle. Older students can work in pairs or small groups, while you might work with younger students to help them complete the puzzle.

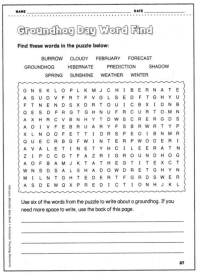

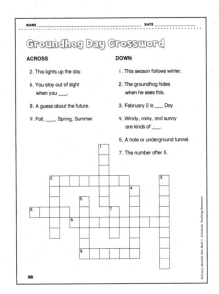

UNDERGROUND BURROW MAZE

Use the maze on page 39 to motivate students to complete assignments or meet other class or individual goals. Once a student has accomplished the pre-established goal, give him or her a copy of the maze. Challenge the student to help the groundhog get to its bed by drawing a line along the path without crossing any of the solid lines within the maze. Once finished, the student can color the pictures, then display the page in an area set up specifically for showing off student work.

WAKE UP, MR. GROUNDHOG!

Use this game for a small-group or learning-center activity. Or, make several copies of the game and divide the class into groups so they can all play at the same time! To get started, photocopy the game boards (pages 40–41). Glue the two parts of the game board together on poster board or to the inside of a file folder. How you use the game and what skills you want students to practice is up to you. Simply write the desired text (or problems) on the spaces of the game board and label a set of task cards (page 42) to use with the game. Then color and laminate the game board and task cards for durability.

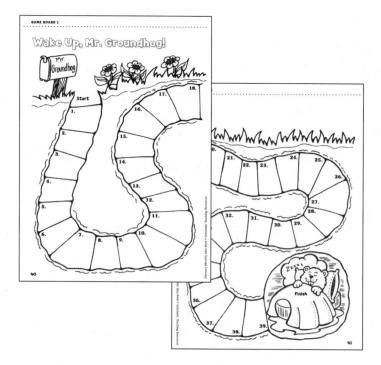

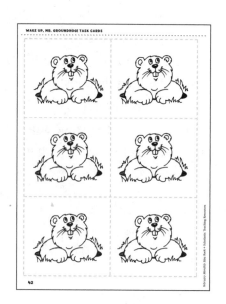

Weather Record Keeper

Date	Sunny	Cloudy	Rainy	Snowy	Windy	Temperature	
						High	Low

Measuring Shadows

I am _____ feet and _____ inches tall.

A friend helped me measure my shadow at different times during the day. This is what I found out.

Time	Length of My Shadow

My shadow was longest at _____.

My shadow was shortest at _____.

Here's something else I noticed about my shadow:

_____

_____

_____

February Monthly Idea Book © Scholastic Teaching Resources

Hibernation Investigation

_____

(Author)

Groundhog Day Word Find

Find these words in the puzzle below:

BURROW   CLOUDY   FEBRUARY   FORECAST

GROUNDHOG   HIBERNATE   PREDICTION   SHADOW

SPRING   SUNSHINE   WEATHER   WINTER

```
G N S K L O P L K M J C H I B E R N A T E
A S U D V F R T F V G L S E D F T G H Y U
F T N E N D S X D R T O U I C B X I D N B
Q E S D F R G T G H N U F R C U R T O M N
A X H R C V B N H Y T D W S C R E R G D S
A O I V F E B R U A R Y F S B R W R T Y P
X L N O O F E T T I D R S P E O I B N M R
Q U E C R B G F W I N T E R P W O D E R I
A V A L E T I N E T Y H C I L E E R A T N
Z I P C C G T F A Z R I G R O U N D H O G
A O F B A M J K T A T H E G T I T E X C T
W N S D S A L S H A D O W D R E T G H Y N
M I L N T G H T E D E R T F G R D S W E R
A S D E W Q X P R E D I C T I O N H J K L
```

Use six of the words from the puzzle to write about a groundhog. If you need more space to write, use the back of this page.

_____

_____

_____

_____

Groundhog Day Crossword

ACROSS

2. This lights up the day.

6. You stay out of sight when you ___.

8. A guess about the future.

9. Fall, ___, Spring, Summer

DOWN

1. This season follows winter.

2. The groundhog hides when he sees this.

3. February 2 is ___ Day.

4. Windy, rainy, and sunny are kinds of ___.

5. A hole or underground tunnel.

7. The number after 5.

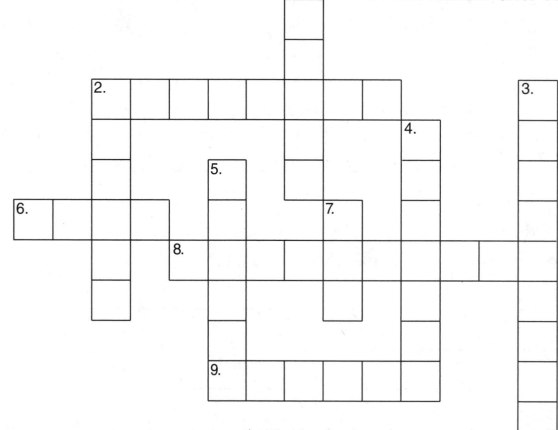

February Monthly Idea Book © Scholastic Teaching Resources

Underground Burrow Maze

Wake Up, Mr. Groundhog!

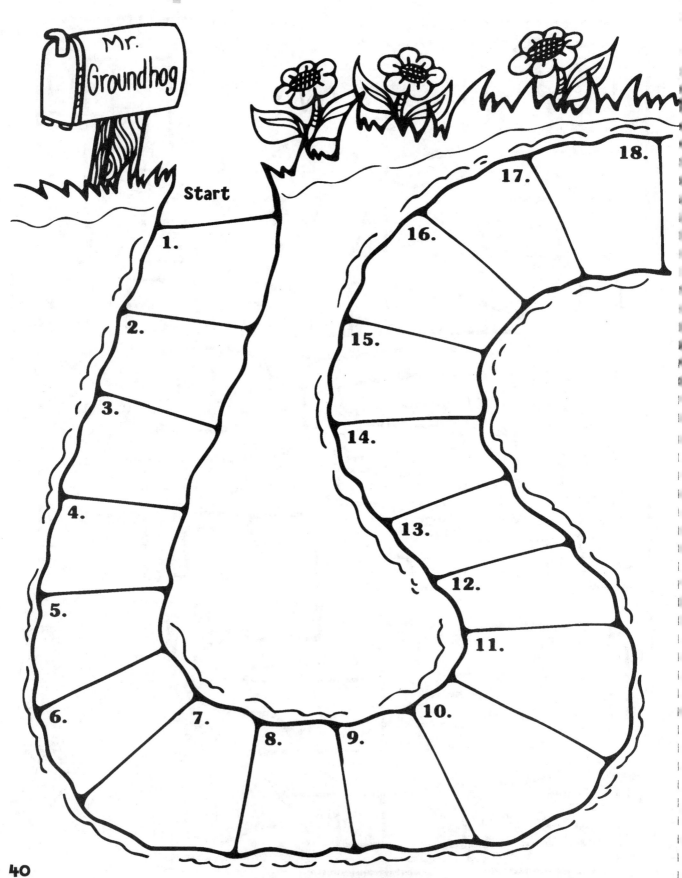

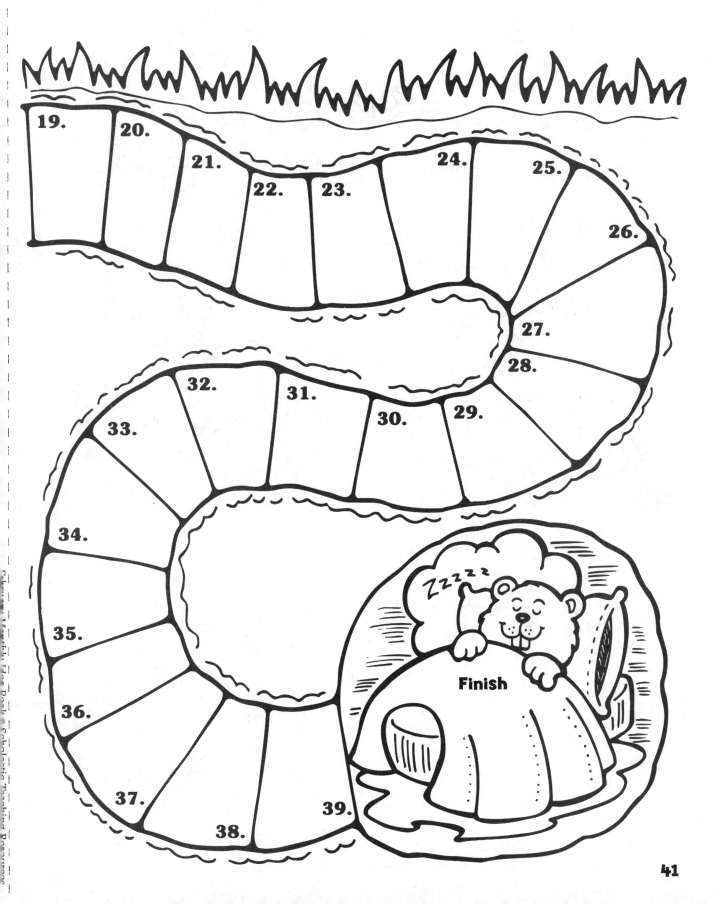

Finish

VALENTINE'S DAY

One of the most fascinating stories that surrounds Valentine's Day is that of Saint Valentine himself. In 269 A.D., a young priest named Valentinus was arrested and imprisoned by the Romans for his religious beliefs and for secretly marrying couples. While in prison, Valentinus befriended the blind daughter of his jailer and is said to have converted both of them to Christianity and even to have restored the young woman's vision. On February 14, the eve of his execution, Valentinus wrote a farewell message to the young woman and signed it "From Your Valentine." Over time, this phrase has become synonymous with expressions of love, friendship, and affection.

Suggested Activities

 ## VALENTINE'S DAY CROSSWORD

Give students practice with Valentine's Day vocabulary and developing problem-solving skills with the crossword puzzle on page 48. Distribute photocopies to students, then demonstrate how to use the clues to find the answers and fill in the puzzle. Older students can work in pairs or small groups, while you might work with younger students to help them complete the puzzle.

 ## IRRESISTIBLE BINGO

Reinforce vocabulary words with a game of Irresistible Bingo! To prepare, make several photocopies of the Bingo game board on page 49. On each page, fill in the vocabulary words you want students to practice, using the same words but in a different arrangement on each game board. Also, write each word on a plain index card. Copy the programmed game boards, making enough for each student in a group (or the whole class) to have one. Laminate the game boards and word cards for durability. To use, supply players with Bingo chips or dried beans to use as markers, then have a caller choose one word card at a time to read to players. If players have that word on their game board, they cover it with a marker. Continue play until players have covered all of the words on their game boards. At that time, all the players call out "Bingo!" together.

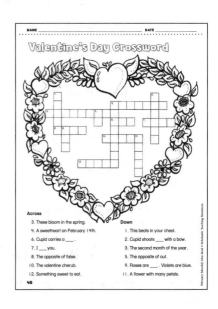

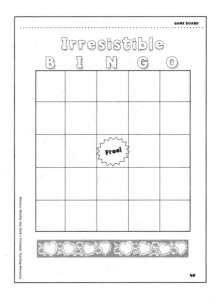

★ JUST-FOR-YOU NOTE

Invite students to create a special note to give to their special valentine on February 14. Distribute red or pink copies of page 50 to students. Then have them cut out the pattern, fold it back along the dashed lines, and cut out the dimple at the top of the heart through both thicknesses. Students can write their message on the lines, then fold the plain heart forward to cover the message. Finally, have them write the name of the card recipient on the front.

★ VALENTINE PICTURE FRAME

This simple picture frame makes a wonderful gift for students to give to their special valentine! To make, ask students to fold a sheet of tagboard in half. Have them cut out the pattern (page 51), glue it to the tagboard along the fold, then cut out the heart-shaped opening from the front of the card only. Finally, help students glue a photo or self-portrait in the opening. They can stand their frame, tent-style, on a flat surface to display their picture.

★ POETRY IN RHYME

Reinforce students' poetry-writing skills with this fun Valentine's Day activity. Distribute a photocopy of Rhyme-Time Valentine (page 52) to students. Explain that they will brainstorm and write words that rhyme with each word listed on the page. Afterward, invite students to share their words and add others to their list, if desired. Then have students write a draft of a rhyming poem on the back of their page, using some of the words from the front. Ask them to compose a poem related to a Valentine's Day theme, such as friendship, love of family, and similar topics. Tell students that their poems can be serious or humorous. When finished, distribute copies of the stationery on page 53 for students to use for their final draft.

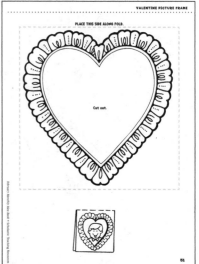

HEART-SHAPED PAGE TOPPER

Celebrate student achievement with Valentine's Day page toppers that are sure to make any bulletin board a hit! Distribute photocopies of the pattern on page 54 to students. To make a topper, ask students to cut out the pattern along the solid lines and fold the wedged sections back along the dotted lines. Have them tape the straight edges of the sections together, then slip the topper over the corner of a page of their work. For added flare, you might provide students with colored copies of the pattern. Or, invite them to use glitter glue, plastic gems, lace, or other craft materials to embellish their page toppers.

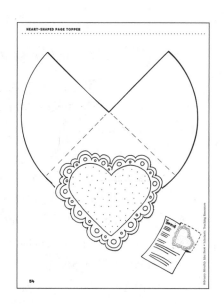

HAPPY HEART GLASSES

Invite students to make and wear a pair of heart-shaped glasses to celebrate Valentine's Day. Distribute copies of the patterns on page 55. Have students color and cut out the patterns, carefully cutting the slits on the glasses frame and the earpieces. To assemble, students simply fit each earpiece into the corresponding slit on the frame. If desired, students can take their glasses home to wear as they deliver their valentine cards, notes, or other messages to family members.

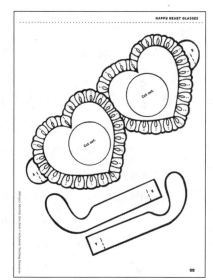

SWEETHEART SKILLS

Reinforce a variety of skills with these hinged hearts. To assemble, cut out construction-paper copies of the patterns on pages 56–57. (Make as many copies as you need for the skill you plan to teach.) Program the two half-hearts with the skill you want to teach and write the answer on the whole heart. Use a brass fastener to assemble the pieces, as shown. To use, students read the task, give their response, then separate the two halves of the heart to check their answer.

If desired, invite students to make their own hinged valentines. They can label the half-heart shapes with a Valentine's Day greeting and write a special message on the whole heart. Or, they might write a riddle and its answer on the pieces.

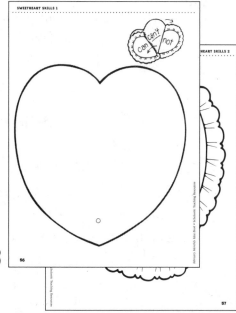

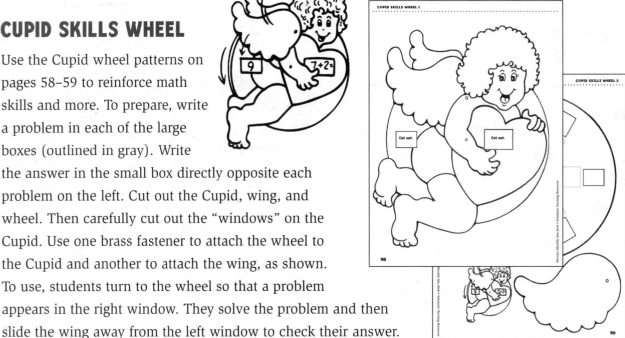

★ CUPID SKILLS WHEEL

Use the Cupid wheel patterns on pages 58–59 to reinforce math skills and more. To prepare, write a problem in each of the large boxes (outlined in gray). Write the answer in the small box directly opposite each problem on the left. Cut out the Cupid, wing, and wheel. Then carefully cut out the "windows" on the Cupid. Use one brass fastener to attach the wheel to the Cupid and another to attach the wing, as shown. To use, students turn to the wheel so that a problem appears in the right window. They solve the problem and then slide the wing away from the left window to check their answer.

★ MAIL CARRIER CAP

Students can don these easy-to-make mail carrier caps as they role-play postal workers delivering heartfelt messages on Valentine's Day. First, provide students with photocopies of the cap pattern (page 60) and 2-inch-wide strips of tagboard that are long enough to fit around students' heads (for use as headbands). To make their caps, give students the following instructions:

1. Color and cut out the cap pattern.

2. Write your name on the cap bill. Then fold the bill up toward the cap.

3. Glue or staple the cap to a strip of tagboard.

4. Ask a classmate to help fit the tagboard around your head, then staple the ends in place.

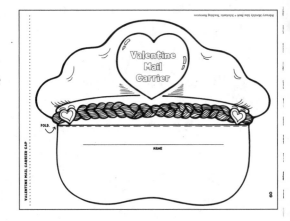

★ SPECIAL DELIVERY TRUCKS

Have students prepare simple mailboxes for use when delivering and collecting their valentines and other mail. Distribute a file folder and photocopy of the truck pattern (page 61) to each student. Ask students to color, cut out, and glue the truck to one side of their

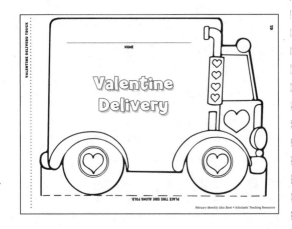

folder. Then help them tape the sides of their folder together to create a large pocket. Display the delivery truck "mailboxes" on a bulletin board within easy reach of students.

★ CUPID CENTERPIECES

Set the tone for a Valentine's Day celebration with these centerpieces that hold special treats inside. You might make and give one to each student. Or you might invite students to make the centerpieces to take home to their families. Depending on for whom the projects are being prepared, you can supply treats such as small toys, pencils, erasers, or individually-wrapped snacks or candy to place inside the centerpieces. To begin, make photocopies of the Cupid pattern on page 62 and do the following to prepare each centerpiece:

1. Color and cut out the Cupid pattern.

2. Bring the straight edge toward the heart, forming a cone from the pattern. Tape the ends together.

3. Put the treat(s) in the open end of the cone. Then tape the cone closed.

★ CLASS PHOTO ALBUM

Take photos of your class Valentine's Day activities to compile into a photo album. Then, throughout the year, add pictures of other class events. No matter the time of year, students will enjoy browsing through the photos of themselves and peers. If desired, invite students to bring in pictures of their own special events. Whether the pictures depict birthday or holiday celebrations, family vacations, or community activities, these photos will make a great supplement to your class album. Be sure to also include pictures of class field trips, special projects, or other adventures that your class has participated in. After arranging the pages of the album, add a cover, such as the one on page 63. Title the cover and add an author line. When completed, invite students to enjoy the photos and share stories about their experiences depicted in the pictures. Add the album to your class library so students can visit it again and again. (Note: Be sure to obtain permission from parents or guardians before adding and showing photos of students and/or their families.)

Valentine's Day Crossword

Across

3. These bloom in the spring.

4. A sweetheart on February 14th.

6. Cupid carries a ____ .

7. I ____ you.

8. The opposite of false.

10. The valentine cherub.

12. Something sweet to eat.

Down

1. This beats in your chest.

2. Cupid shoots ____ with a bow.

3. The second month of the year.

5. The opposite of out.

9. Roses are ____ . Violets are blue.

11. A flower with many petals.

Irresistible
BINGO

Free!

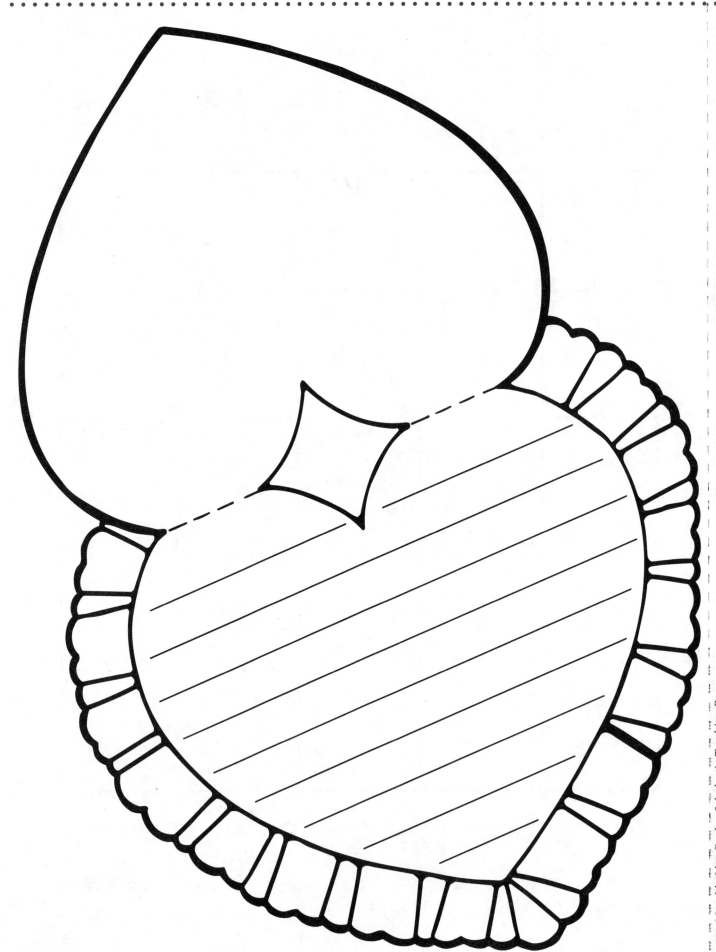

PLACE THIS SIDE ALONG FOLD.

Cut out.

Rhyme-Time Valentine

**Write as many rhyming words as possible
to go with each of the words below.**

dear _____

_____

sweet _____

_____

day _____

_____

red _____

_____

love _____

_____

see _____

_____

mine _____

_____

February Monthly Idea Book © Scholastic Teaching Resources

Hug · Good Kid · Pals · Love · Sweet · Hug · Love

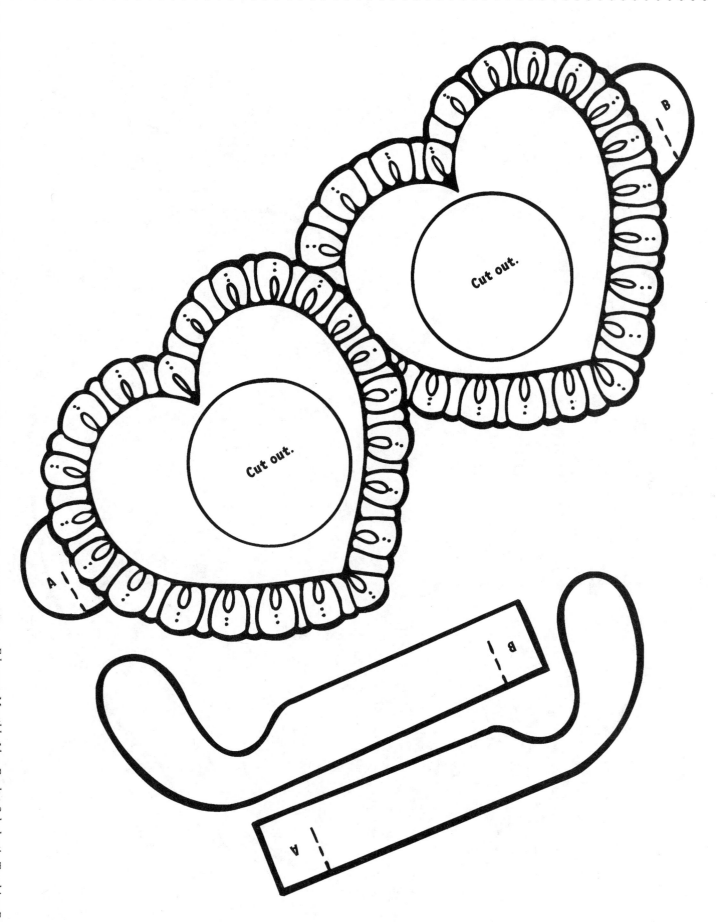

can can't not

○

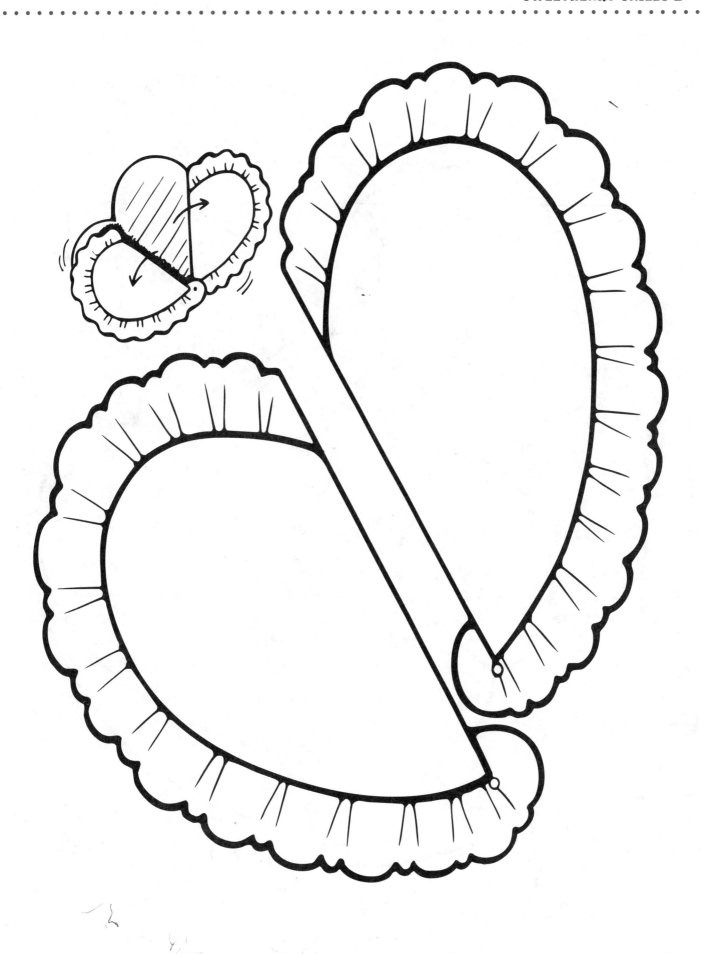

Cut out.

Cut out.

February Monthly-Idea Book © Scholastic Teaching Resources

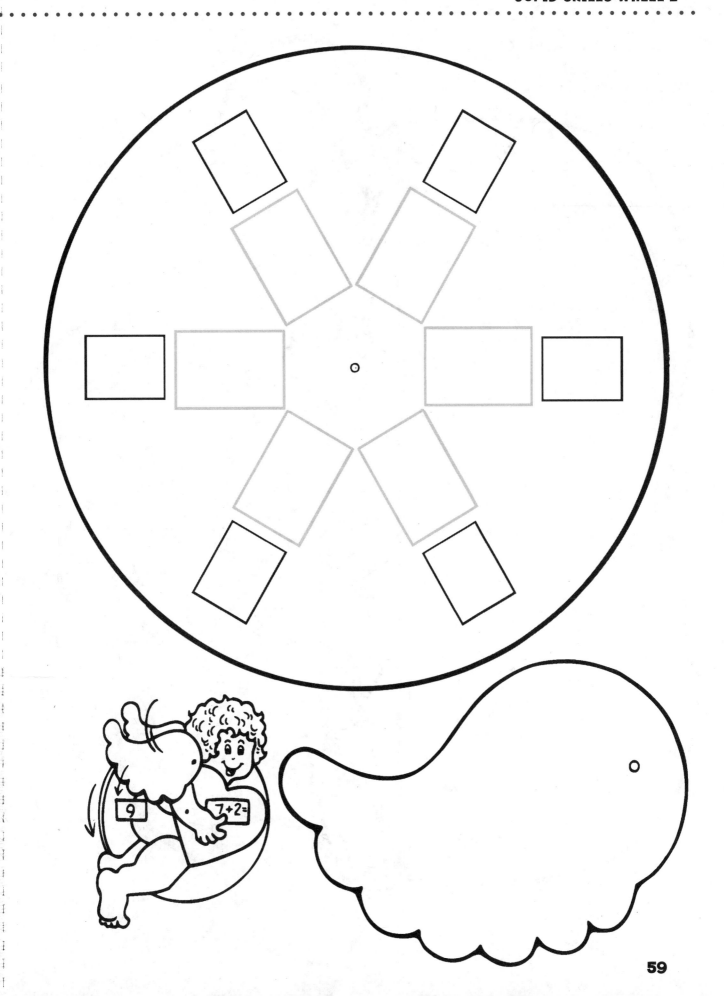

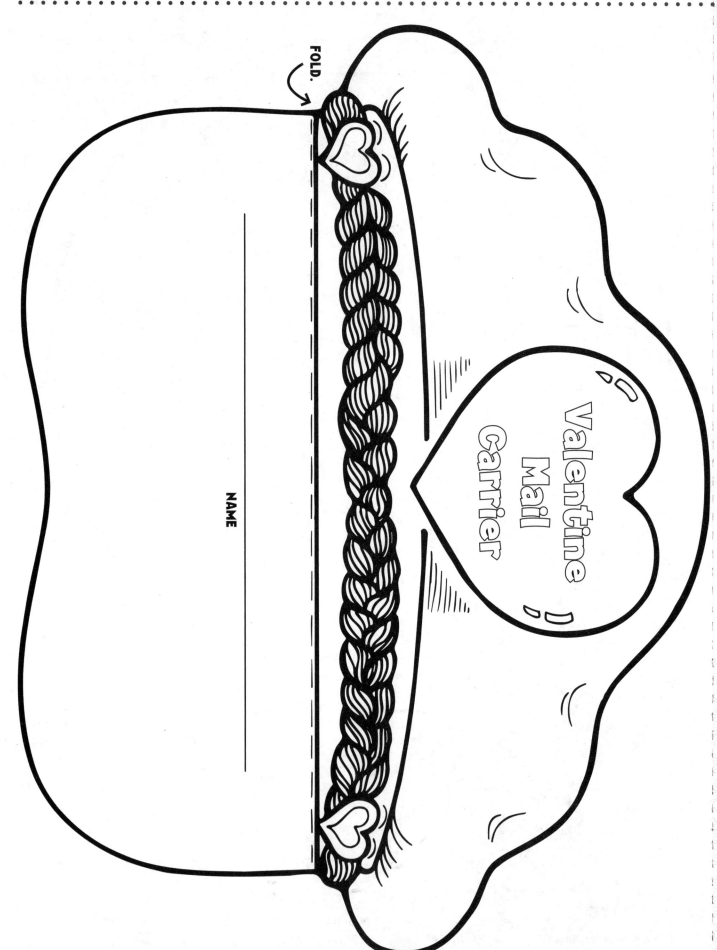

FOLD.

NAME

Valentine Mail Carrier

PLACE THIS SIDE ALONG FOLD.

Valentine
Delivery

NAME

NAME

February Monthly Idea Book © Scholastic Teaching Resources

PLACE THIS SIDE ALONG FOLD.

HEART HEALTH

Kick off National Heart Month by helping students learn about the function, anatomy, and care of the human heart. Located in the middle of the chest and just behind the breastbone, the heart muscle is about the size of a closed fist. The heart grows as a person grows and expands and contracts to pump blood to every part of the body.

Suggested Activities

★ PARTS-OF-A-HEART DIAGRAM

Distribute a photocopy of the heart diagram (page 68) to each student. Point out that the diagram shows how the heart would look from the perspective of the patient, not the viewer. To illustrate, have students hold their pages against their chests with the text facing outward and explain that the diagram shows how their heart would look inside their body.

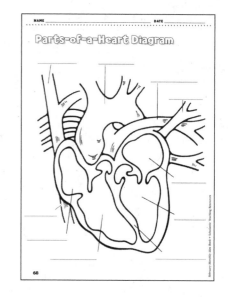

As a class, discuss the following parts of the heart and their corresponding locations and functions: *superior vena cava, aorta, pulmonary artery, pulmonary vein, left atrium, left ventricle, septum, right ventricle, right atrium,* and *inferior vena cava.* Explain that the heart is divided into four chambers: the left and right atriums (upper sections) and ventricles (lower sections). Then tell students that the left ventricle pumps oxygen-rich blood through the arteries to the entire body. The right ventricle pumps oxygen-depleted blood to the lungs, where it becomes oxygenated. After sharing this information, work with small groups to fill in the diagram and discuss the different parts of the heart. You can check the answers to the diagram on page 143.

★ COUNT THE BEATS!

Help students discover that their heartbeat (or pulse) increases with exercise and decreases with rest. First, pair up students and give a photocopy of the record sheet (page 69) to each student. Explain that the partners will take turns doing the following to take their pulse rates at rest and after a brief period of exercise:

1. One student locates his or her own pulse on either the wrist or neck. The student should use his or her fingertips (not thumb) to feel the pulse.

2. On a signal, the student's partner measures 20 seconds using a stopwatch or a watch with a second hand. During this time, the first student counts the number of times his or her pulse throbs. Each throb represents a beat of the heart. At the end of the time interval, the student records the findings on his or her record sheet.

3. Next, The first student jogs in place for two minutes while his or her partner times the action. (Jogging will speed up the student's heart rate.)

4. After jogging, the partners repeat step 2.

5. The partners switch roles and repeat steps 1–4.

6. Finally, each student uses the back of his or her page to write about ways to have a healthy heart.

After every student has done the activity and completed a record sheet, gather the class together to share their results. Discuss how the heart rate differs when the heart is at rest versus after a period of exercise. Explain that exercise makes the heart work harder, causing it to beat at a faster rate. Invite volunteers to share their own insights about how exercise and nutritional choices relate to a healthy heart. If desired, take this opportunity to share other heart-related facts with students, such as that the average adult's heart beats about 60 to 100 times a minute and pumps about five liters of blood per minute, and the heart of a 4- to 8-year-old child beats 90–100 times per minute.

HEART-SMART MOBILE

After discussing different things students can do to keep their hearts and bodies healthy, distribute photocopies of the mobile patterns on pages 70–71. Also provide two-foot lengths of yarn, scissors, and a hole punch. Then invite students to follow these directions to make a mobile:

1. Cut out the large and small heart patterns.

2. Record your ideas about ways to keep your heart healthy on the back of each small heart. Write ideas that correspond to the text on the front of each heart. For example, on the back of the heart labeled "Eat a Balanced Diet," you might write a list of heart-healthy foods.

3. Punch a hole in the top of each heart pattern where indicated.

4. Cut a two-foot length of yarn into four pieces of varying lengths. Then tie one piece of yarn to the hole in each small heart. Tie the other end of each piece of yarn to a hole in the bottom of the large heart.

5. Thread the last length of yarn through the hole in the top of the large heart and tie the ends together to make a hanger for the mobile.

After students complete their mobiles, hang them in the classroom to serve as a reminder of some ways to maintain a healthy heart. Or, send the mobiles home with students to share with families.

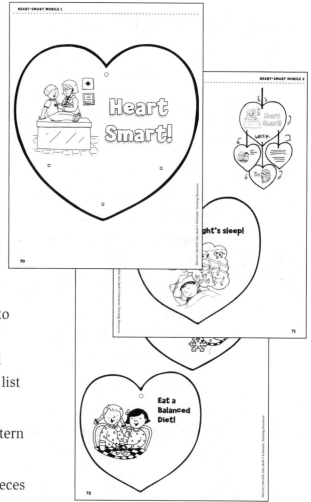

★ MR. HEARTBEAT STICK PUPPET

Photocopy and distribute the heart puppet patterns (pages 73–74) to students. Ask students to color and cut out their patterns, then draw a large face on the heart cutout. Next, have them use five brass fasteners, where indicated on the patterns, to assemble their puppets. If desired, invite students to glue a wide craft stick to the back of Mr. Heartbeat's body to use as a puppet handle. They can move their puppet in a variety of ways to make it dance or to spin and wiggle its limbs in amusing ways. To reinforce good behavior or reward completing assignments, you might award one part of the heart puppet at a time to students when they meet an established goal. Once a student has collected all six pieces, he or she can then assemble the puppet.

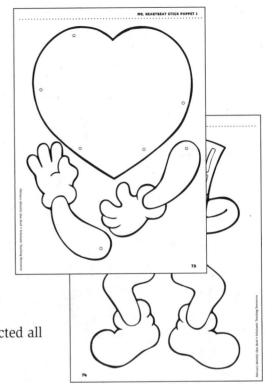

★ HEALTHY RESEARCH

Encourage students to research the kinds of eating, sleeping, and exercise habits that can help keep their hearts healthy. Explain that each member of the class can use books available in the school or public library, Internet resources, and other sources, such as personal interviews, to do their research. (Most students will need a few days to complete the assignment.)

   After students complete their research and have written their reports, distribute photocopies of the report cover on page 75. Ask students to color the pictures and write their name on the line provided to complete the sentence. Then have them stack their report pages behind the cover and staple together. Afterward, invite volunteers to share their report with the class.

Parts-of-a-Heart Diagram

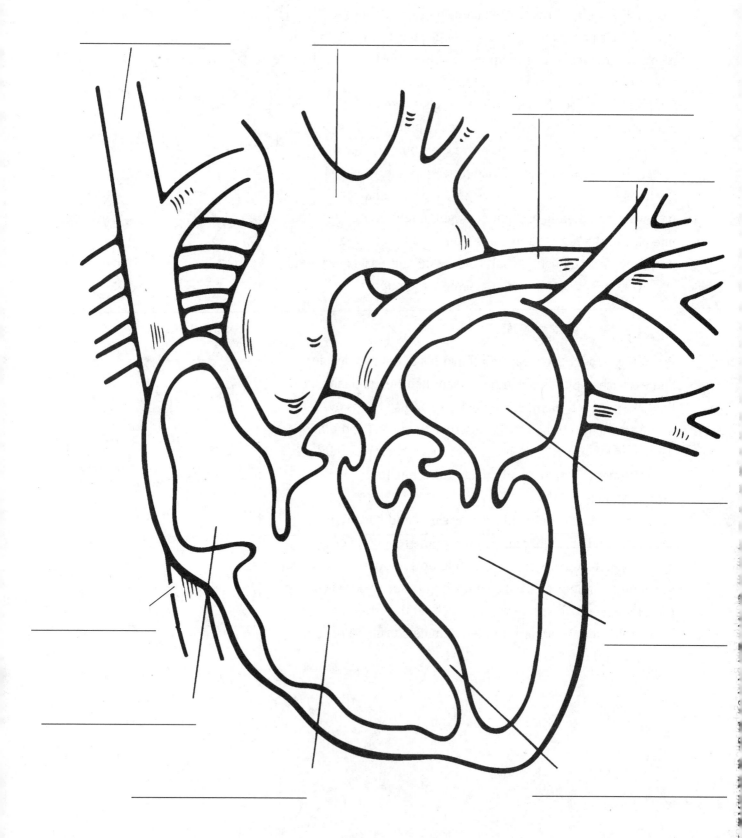

Count the Beats! Record Sheet

1. The human heart is an important muscle in the human body. Write three facts you know about the heart.

   _____

   _____

   _____

2. Find your own pulse at your wrist or on your neck under the jaw. Ask your partner to keep time for 20 seconds while you count the number of times your heart beats (at the pulse point you've chosen).

   I counted _____ heartbeats in 20 seconds.

   Now, multiply the number above by three. This will tell you how many times your heart beats per minute. Complete the sentence:

   When I'm resting, my heart beats _____ times in one minute.

3. Next, jog in place for two minutes. Then ask your partner to keep time again for 20 seconds while you count your heartbeats.

   I counted _____ heartbeats in 20 seconds.

   Now, multiply that number by three and complete the sentence:

   When I'm exercising, my heart beats _____ times in one minute.

4. Use the back of this page to write about some ways you can keep your heart healthy.

Heart Smart!

Larry

Eat a Balanced Diet!

Get Plenty of Exercise!

Get a good night's sleep!

Get
Plenty of
Exercise!

Eat a
Balanced
Diet!

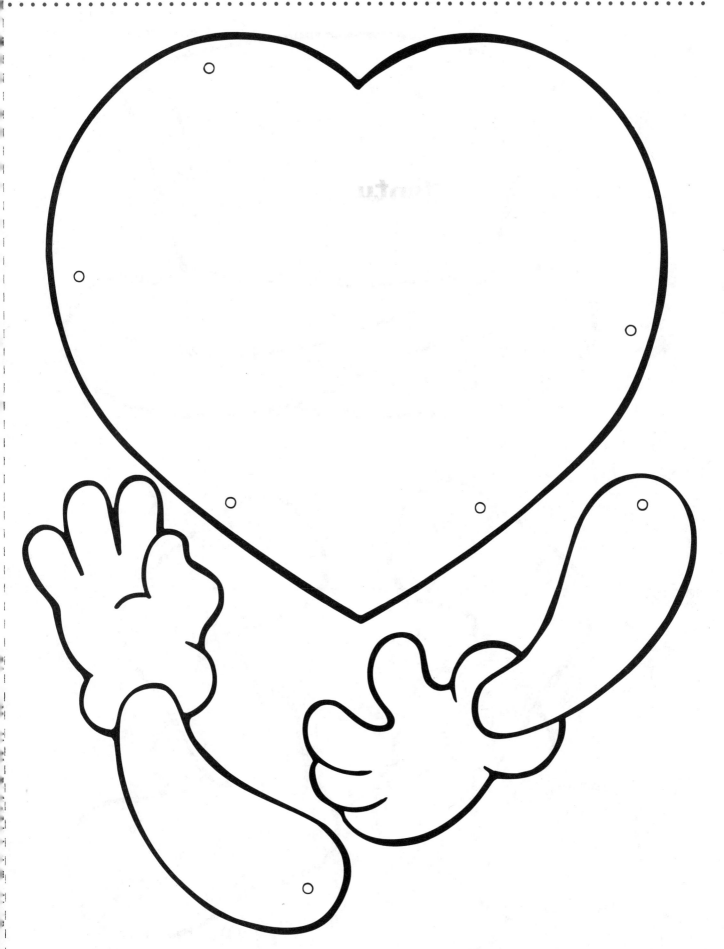

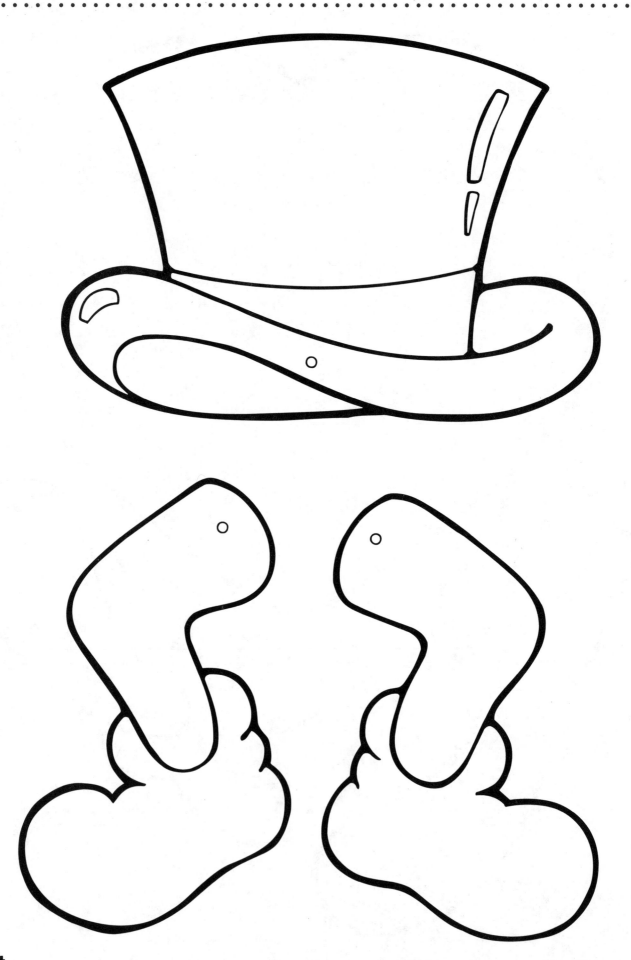

February Monthly Idea Book © Scholastic Teaching Resources

Have a Healthy Heart!

_____

knows that good nutrition, exercise, and plenty of sleep
help make a healthy heart and body.

PRESIDENTS' DAY

While celebrated each year on the third Monday in February as a tribute to former American presidents, the holiday known as Presidents' Day began as a way to acknowledge the historical legacies of Presidents George Washington and Abraham Lincoln.

George Washington

After America won its independence from England, George Washington was elected (in 1789) and served as the first president of the United States. His reputation as Commander-in-Chief of the Continental Army had helped secure his place in history as a man of honesty, strength, and leadership. In fact, Washington was considered so honest that a legendary story developed about how he would not lie about chopping down a cherry tree when he was a child. The capital of the United States, as well as many cities across the nation, is named in honor of George Washington.

Abraham Lincoln

In 1834, Abraham Lincoln was elected to the House of Representatives. He went on to become a senator for Illinois. In 1860, Americans voted for Lincoln to serve as the 16th president of the United States. Lincoln was president during the Civil War, when the North and South fought over many issues, including slavery. One of his best-known speeches from that time is the *Gettysburg Address*.

Suggested Activities

 PRESIDENTS' DAY WORD FIND

Use the word find on page 84 to help students become familiar with president-related vocabulary. After students complete the activity, have them use words from the puzzle in a creative writing exercise.

★ COMMANDER-IN-CHIEF REPORT

Have students complete the fill-in report sheets on pages 85–86 as they research and learn more about George Washington and Abraham Lincoln. (You might make two-sided copies of the report sheets.) They can use resources available in the classroom as well as library books, Internet sources, videos, and so on. Students might visit the website for the Smithsonian National Museum of American History (*The American Presidency: A Glorious Burden*) at www.americanhistory.si.edu/presidency/home.html for some useful information.

When students complete their research, invite volunteers to share their discoveries with the class. Then form small groups and assign either President Washington or President Lincoln to each group. Explain that the students will take a closer look at a specific facet of their president, or research American life and culture during his presidency. For example, one group might learn about Washington's military career. Another group might research American industry and trade during Lincoln's term as president. You might read aloud level-appropriate books about Washington and Lincoln to younger students, then ask them to share what they have learned. They can also write and/or draw about related information that they find interesting.

After the groups have compiled their findings, invite them to make visual aids to accompany their reports. They can create props, such as puppets, posters, or scenery. (Descriptions of several prop and puppet patterns are included on pages 81 and 82 for student use.) Or, groups might want to develop creative ways to present their information. For example, they might write a poem, skit, or song to incorporate in their presentation. Finally, have the groups share their presentations with the class.

COMMANDER-IN-CHIEF CONCENTRATION

Help students learn the names of the U.S. Presidents from George Washington to the present with this simple game. First photocopy two sets of the president cards on pages 87–97. (Blank cards are provided on page 98 that can be filled out and used for future presidents.) Choose 12–15 card pairs to use for the game. Shuffle the cards and place them facedown to form a grid. Then invite student pairs or small groups to play the game. Have students take turns flipping over two cards at a time in search of matching cards. If students find a match, they keep the pair. If not, they return the cards facedown to the grid. The game ends when all of the matches have been found. The player with the most matches wins the game.

For a variation, you might use only one card per president, then create a set of text cards identical in size and shape to the president cards. On each text card, label a fact or accomplishment associated with a different president. To play, students try to match each president to the corresponding fact.

NAME THAT PRESIDENT!

Before having students play this presidential guessing game, cut out the pictures of George Washington on page 87 and Abraham Lincoln on page 90. Tape each cutout to a separate headband. Then photocopy a class set of pages 99–100. Distribute the president reference pages to students and review the facts shown for each president. Then ask students to research library books, Internet sites, or other sources to discover more interesting information to add to their reference pages.

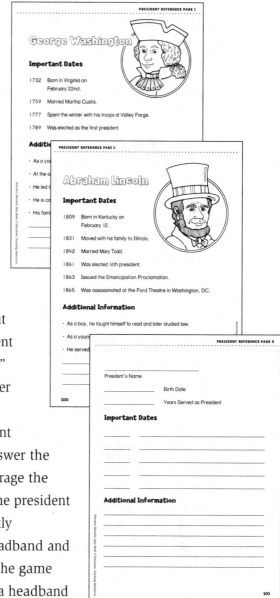

After students complete their pages, divide the class into small groups, and invite one group at a time to play the game. Explain that, to play, a student will put on one of the headbands, without looking at the president pictured on it. That student will then ask "yes" and "no" questions about the identity of the president on his or her headband. For instance, the student might ask "Was the president a military leader?" or "Did he serve as president during the Civil War?" Members of the group should answer the questions, using their reference pages as a guide. Encourage the student in the headband to try to guess the identity of the president using as few clues as possible. Once that student correctly identifies the president, invite another child to don a headband and ask questions about the "mystery" president. Continue the game until every student in the group has had a turn to wear a headband and guess the president pictured on it.

If desired, take the game further by having students fill in the blanks on copies of page 101 to create reference pages for different presidents. Students can choose a president, cut out a copy of his picture (from pages 87–97) to glue to the page, then research their president and write their findings to complete the reference page. Also, have students color and cut out a second picture of their president to tape to a headband. Before playing the game with small groups, invite students to share their presidential findings with the group. (You might also copy each student's reference page to distribute to the other group members.) Then play the game, using the student-made headbands and reference pages. Afterward, you can compile a reference page for each president into a collaborative book about American presidents to add to your class library.

★ "PRESIDENTIAL" EAGLES

Making this majestic bird is a great way to introduce the eagle's place on our nation's Presidential Seal. First, provide each student with photocopies of the eagle patterns (pages 102–103), a small paper bag, a rubber band, and shredded paper (the school office will likely have plenty to offer). To make the eagle, have students do the following:

1. Fill the bag about two-thirds full with shredded paper. Twist the open end of the bag to close it, then secure with the rubber band.

2. Color and cut out the eagle patterns. Glue the cutouts to the bag, as shown.

After students complete their eagles, invite them to display their birds on a class bulletin board along with a picture, report, or fact sheet about their favorite president.

★ GETTING THE *GETTYSBURG ADDRESS*

After the secession of southern states from the Union, Lincoln spoke in Pennsylvania at what was to be the dedication of a cemetery for thousands of men who lost their lives in the Battle of Gettysburg. This brief, two-minute speech—known as Lincoln's *Gettysburg Address*—had an important impact on the course of our country and is considered one of the most famous speeches in American history.

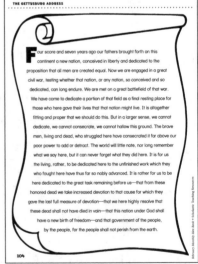

To help make the content of this important speech understandable to students, distribute photocopies of page 104 to the class. Explain to students that the text on their page contains the words to the *Gettysburg Address*. Then read the speech aloud as students follow along on their copies. As you read, pause after every few sentences, inviting students to discuss what has been read and to share their understanding of what Lincoln meant by his words.

Afterward, work with the class to rewrite Lincoln's speech, using students' own words to create a modern-day version. You might use an interactive whiteboard for this exercise to make editing and correcting easier to do as you go along. When the draft of the class version is complete, talk with students about strategies they used to complete their rewrite, such as discussing word meanings, considering context, and summarizing to better express a concept or idea. Finally, have students make a hand-copy of the class version of the *Gettysburg Address* to share with others. If desired, have students practice performing the speech in front of small groups, then challenge them to present the speech to family members and others in the community.

★PRESIDENTIAL PROPS

Invite students to make some of the following props to enhance their learning and role-playing. Three-cornered caps conjure up images of George Washington and his contemporaries. Hats, beards, and log cabins are synonymous with stories about and images of Abraham Lincoln. Stand-up characters and puppets of both historical figures will challenge students to take presentations and read-alouds further, encouraging them to add visual interest and dramatic elements.

Washington's Three-Cornered Hat

Make three photocopies of the hat and star patterns (page 105) for each student. Have students color and cut out each of their patterns. Then, to assemble, help them staple the three hat cutouts together, as shown, to form the three-cornered hat. Students can glue a star near each corner of their hat for decoration.

Stovepipe Hat

Give each student a 18- by 22-inch sheet of black construction paper and a 14-inch black paper circle. Also, provide a few 6-inch tagboard circles for students to use as tracers. To make a Lincoln-like stovepipe hat, have students do the following:

1. Tape the short ends of the rectangular sheet of paper together to form a cylinder, as shown. This will be the tall part of the hat.

2. To make the brim, trace the 6-inch tagboard circle onto the center of the black circle. Cut out the smaller circle. Then cut notches around the inner circle, as shown.

3. Fold up the notches in the brim and tape them to the inside of the hat.

Look-Like-Lincoln Beard

Distribute photocopies of the beard pattern (page 106) to students. Have them color and cut out their patterns. To wear, students simply loop the ends of the beard around their ears. This prop works well when paired with the stovepipe hat (page 81).

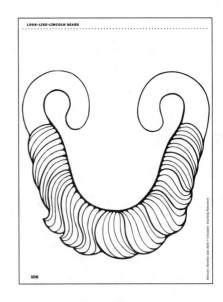

Lincoln's Log Cabin

Invite students to color and cut out photocopies of the log cabin patterns on page 107. Then have them carefully cut along the solid window lines and fold back the two flaps to create a window that can be opened and closed. To complete their log cabin, ask students to glue the chimney to the left side of the house. If desired, invite students to glue pretzel sticks along the clapboard lines of their house to create a more realistic-looking log cabin. They might also back the window with a piece of paper, then open the window flaps and draw a picture of young Abe Lincoln, or another picture to depict a person or scene from Lincoln's log-cabin era.

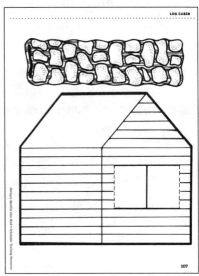

Washington & Lincoln Finger Puppets

To make these quick-and-easy finger puppets, photocopy one pattern of each president puppet (page 108) for each student. Then have students color and cut out their puppets. Help them, as needed, to cut out the small circles on each one. To use, students simply slip their fingers into the holes and wiggle them around to serve as legs for their puppet characters.

★ STAND-UP PRESIDENT PAGE FRAMERS

Students can use the patterns on pages 109 and 110 to create a display for their reports or other writing assignments about presidents. Distribute photocopies of the patterns to students along with 9- by 12-inch sheets of construction paper and pieces of cardboard. To make a stand-up president, have students do the following:

1. Color and cut out the patterns.

2. For each president, glue the head, hands, and feet to the edges of a sheet of construction paper, as shown.

3. For a stand, cut out a triangle from cardboard. Fold back one long edge of the triangle to make a tab, then glue the tab to the back of the page framer.

4. Attach your report or other written work to the front of the page framer. Then stand the framer on a flat surface.

★ SNAPSHOTS OF LESSONS LEARNED

Invite students to revisit their research, Commander-in-Chief reports (see page 77), and President Reference pages (see page 79) to prepare for writing their own thoughts and ideas about George Washington and Abraham Lincoln. Encourage students to be creative as they decide what they want to write and how they want to convey their thoughts. For example, they might write a poem, song, or skit to share information about each president. As they write, remind students to draw from the information they have previously gathered about each president as well as from class discussions and peer presentations. When students are ready to write their final copies, distribute photocopies of the stationery on pages 111 and 112 and have them write about each president on the corresponding page.

After students complete their written work, distribute photocopies of the book cover on page 113. Invite them to color the cover, fill in the author line, and staple their pages to the back of the cover.

Presidents' Day Word Find

ADDRESS   COMMANDER   CONGRESS   CONSTITUTION

ELECTION   INAUGURATION   LEADERSHIP   MILITARY

OVAL OFFICE   PRESIDENT   WASHINGTON   WHITE HOUSE

```
I N M L L R P L K M I N H G A S W E R T X
N S W E L E C T I O N E S L D F T G W Y U
A T I A N P S O V A L O F F I C E I A N B
U E S D F R G T G C E Y F G C O R T S M N
G M E E C E B N H O P E W I C N V R H D S
U I C R F S B R U M T Y F S B S F S I Y P
R L L S O I E T T M N R S R E T R E N M X
A I E H R D G F W A K T E A P I G N G R I
T T R I E E I N E N E H C T L T I A T T N
I A P P C N T F A D N I G V O U R T O O G
O R F B A T J K H E C L W R A T X O N C T
N Y S D S W A D D R E S S D R I A R G Y N
M I L N T V H T E D E R T F G O W S W E R
A W H I T E H O U S E I C C O N G R E S S
```

Using six of the words from the puzzle, write about what you would do if you were president. If you need more space to write, use the back of this page.

_____

_____

_____

_____

Commander-in-Chief Report

This is my president's full name (first, middle, and last):

_____

Did this president have a nickname?   Yes ❑   No ❑

If so, what was it?_____

Birth Date _____

(This is a picture of my president.)

Birthplace _____

What year did this
president take office?_____

How old was he or she? _____

Was he or she elected? Yes ❑   No ❑

If you checked "no," explain how this person
became president.

_____

Who was the vice president? _____

Was this president married? Yes ❑   No ❑

Spouse's Name:

_____

Commander-in-Chief Report (continued)

Describe this president's family.

_____

_____

_____

Name one major national event that happened during this president's term in office.

_____

He or she is famous for many things. Here are a few:

1. _____

2. _____

3. _____

Here are some interesting facts about this president:

_____

_____

_____

 Write a letter to this president on another sheet of paper. What do you think of his or her accomplishments? Explain your opinions. Make suggestions about what this president could have done differently.

1st George Washington
1789–1797

2nd John Adams
1797–1801

3rd Thomas Jefferson
1801–1809

4th James Madison
1809–1817

5th James Monroe
1817–1825

6th John Quincy Adams
1825–1829

7th Andrew Jackson
1829–1837

8th Martin Van Buren
1837–1841

February Monthly Idea Book © Scholastic Teaching Resources

9th William Henry Harrison
1841

10th John Tyler
1841–1845

11th James K. Polk
1845–1849

12th Zachary Taylor
1849–1850

13th Millard Fillmore
1850–1853

14th Franklin Pierce
1853–1857

15th James Buchanan
1857–1861

16th Abraham Lincoln
1861–1865

17th Andrew Johnson
1865–1869

18th Ulysses S. Grant
1869–1877

19th Rutherford B. Hayes
1877–1881

20th James Garfield
1881

21st Chester A. Arthur
1881–1885

22nd Grover Cleveland
1885–1889

23rd Benjamin Harrison
1889–1893

24th Grover Cleveland
1893–1897

25th William McKinley
1897-1901

26th Theodore Roosevelt
1901-1909

27th William Howard Taft
1909-1913

28th Woodrow Wilson
1913-1921

29th Warren G. Harding
1921–1923

30th Calvin Coolidge
1923–1929

31st Herbert Hoover
1929–1933

32nd Franklin D. Roosevelt
1933–1945

33rd Harry S. Truman
1945–1953

34th Dwight D. Eisenhower
1953–1961

35th John F. Kennedy
1961–1963

36th Lyndon B. Johnson
1963–1969

37th Richard M. Nixon
1969–1974

38th Gerald R. Ford
1974–1977

39th James Carter
1977–1981

40th Ronald Reagan
1981–1989

41st *George H. W. Bush*
1989–1993

42nd *William J. Clinton*
1993–2001

43rd *George W. Bush*
2001–2009

44th *Barack Obama*
2009–_____

45th _____
_____

46th _____
_____

47th _____
_____

48th _____
_____

George Washington

Important Dates

1732   Born in Virginia on
        February 22nd.

1759   Married Martha Custis.

1777   Spent the winter with his troops at Valley Forge.

1789   Was elected as the first president.

Additional Information

· As a young man, he studied geography and mathematics.

· At the age of 17, he became a land surveyor.

· He led the Continental Army during the American Revolutionary War.

· He is considered "The Father of Our Country."

· His family lived on a plantation in Virginia called Mount Vernon.

_____

_____

_____

Abraham Lincoln

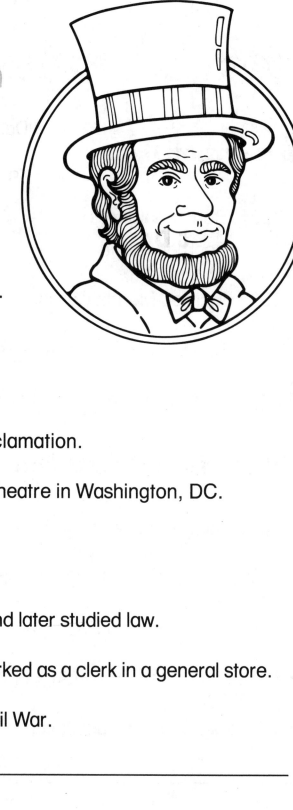

Important Dates

1809   Born in Kentucky on
           February 12.

1831   Moved with his family to Illinois.

1842   Married Mary Todd.

1861   Was elected 16th president.

1863   Issued the Emancipation Proclamation.

1865   Was assassinated at Ford's Theatre in Washington, DC.

Additional Information

· As a boy, he taught himself to read and later studied law.

· As a young man, he split rails and worked as a clerk in a general store.

· He served as president during the Civil War.

_____

_____

_____

_____

President's Name

_____   Birth Date

_____   Years Served as President

Important Dates

_____   _____

_____   _____

_____   _____

_____   _____

_____   _____

Additional Information

_____

_____

_____

_____

_____

_____

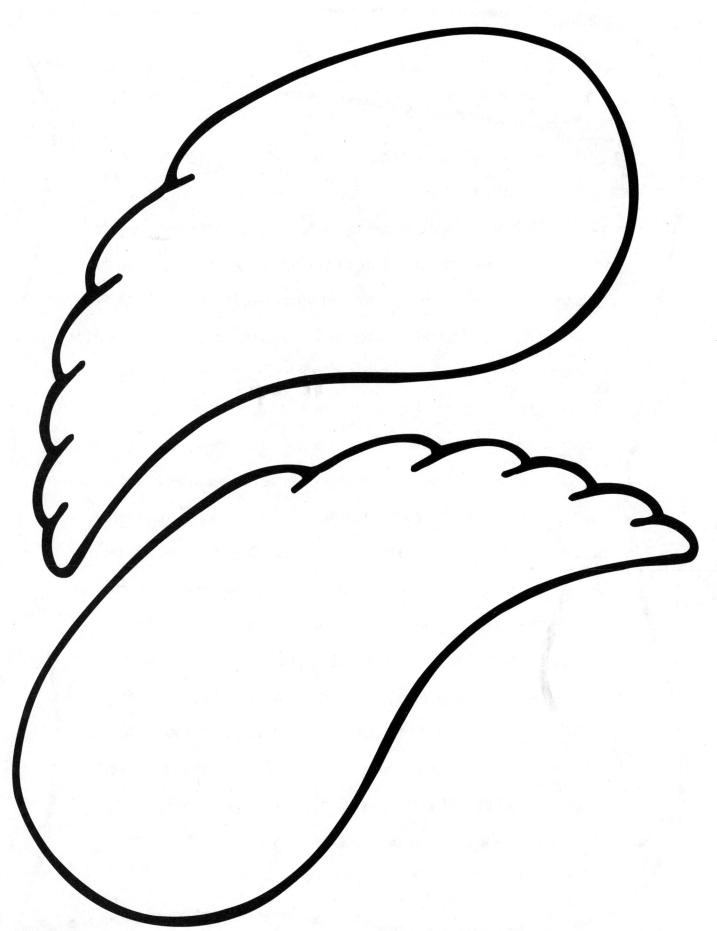

Four score and seven years ago our fathers brought forth on this continent a new nation, conceived in liberty and dedicated to the proposition that all men are created equal. Now we are engaged in a great civil war, testing whether that nation, or any nation, so conceived and so dedicated, can long endure. We are met on a great battlefield of that war. We have come to dedicate a portion of that field as a final resting place for those who here gave their lives that that nation might live. It is altogether fitting and proper that we should do this. But in a larger sense, we cannot dedicate, we cannot consecrate, we cannot hallow this ground. The brave men, living and dead, who struggled here have consecrated it far above our poor power to add or detract. The world will little note, nor long remember what we say here, but it can never forget what they did here. It is for us the living, rather, to be dedicated here to the unfinished work which they who fought here have thus far so nobly advanced. It is rather for us to be here dedicated to the great task remaining before us—that from these honored dead we take increased devotion to that cause for which they gave the last full measure of devotion—that we here highly resolve that these dead shall not have died in vain—that this nation under God shall have a new birth of freedom—and that government of the people, by the people, for the people shall not perish from the earth.

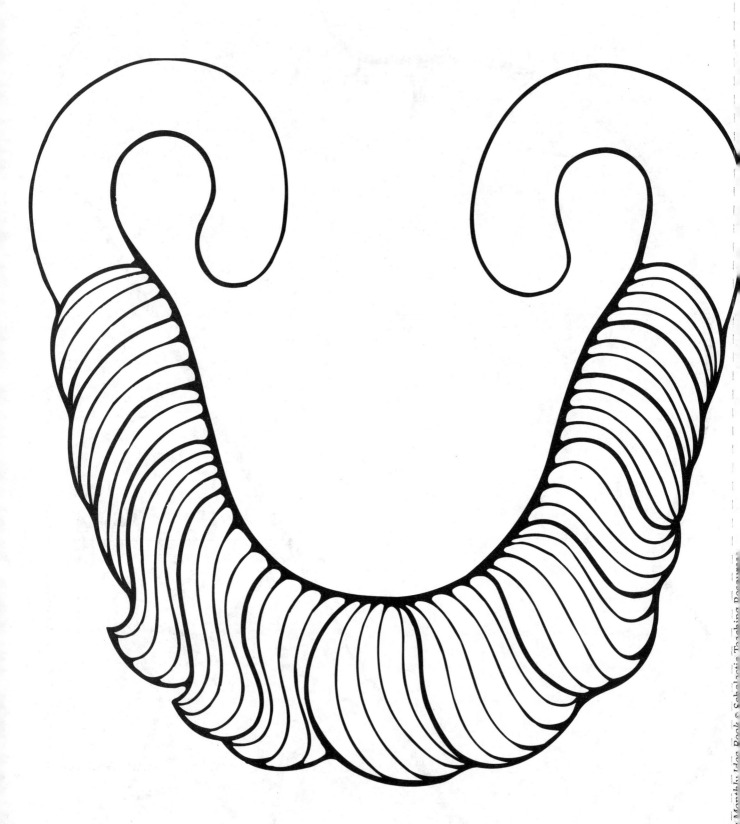

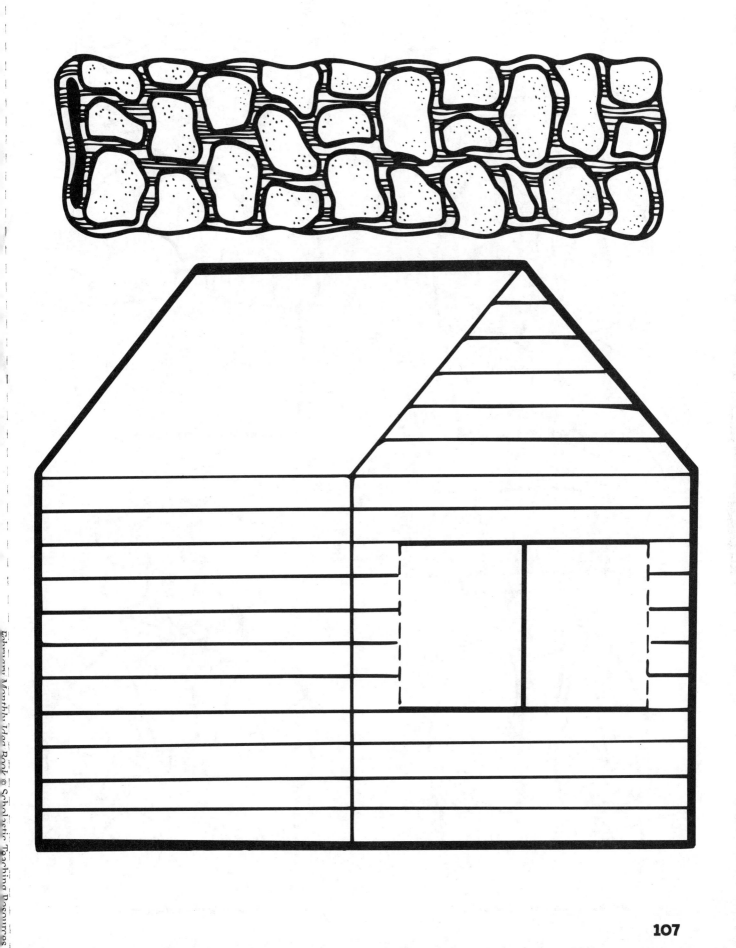

Cut out. Cut out.

Cut out. Cut out.

Cut out. Cut out.

Cut out. Cut out.

I Know My Presidents

by _____

February Monthly Idea Book © Scholastic Teaching Resources

AFRICAN AMERICAN ACHIEVEMENT

The collective success of all Americans is one of many things that make our country a remarkable place to live. Since its beginnings, the United States has depended on and benefited from the intellect, labor, and accomplishments of Americans of color. As students explore the theme of African American achievement in your classroom, talk about the past, present, and future of all Americans.

Suggested Activities

THE CONTRIBUTIONS ACTIVITY

Use this game for a small-group or learning-center activity to help build students awareness of the contributions African Americans have made to our country. For each game set, make photocopies of the activity board and cards on pages 117–119. Then color, cut out, and laminate the pieces. Place the cards in a paper bag. (If desired, make more cards for the activity by labeling the blank cards on page 120 with additional names of famous African Americans, such as Condoleezza Rice, Colin Powell, and Spike Lee.)

Before students do the activity, review each name on the cards and share about that person's accomplishments and the contributions he or she has made to our country. Also, review the different categories on the activity board, providing examples of accomplishments that might fall under each one. Then have small groups follow these directions for the activity:

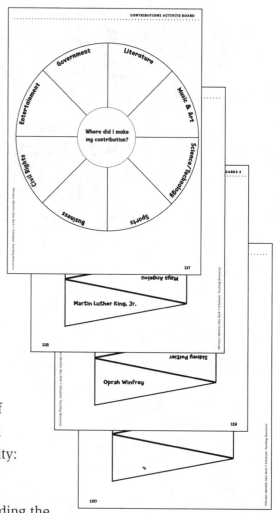

1. Place the activity board in the center of a table.

2. Take turns drawing a card from the bag and reading the name aloud. Look over the areas of achievement on the activity board and decide which category that person's contributions best fit into. (If a name fits more than one category, choose the one you'd like to place the name with.) Tell the group about the person's contribution and to which category it belongs.

3. Place the card near the rim of the activity board circle, with the narrow end of the card pointing to the chosen category.

4. Continue taking turns until all of the cards have been used and placed with a category on the board. As the activity goes on, students can match more than one card to a category, and the cards can even be stacked, if needed.

★ IMPORTANT AMERICAN MINI-BOOK

Provide each student with two-sided photocopies of the mini-book patterns (pages 121–122). Explain that students will use a variety of sources—such as library books, the Internet, and magazine articles—to research famous African Americans, such as Jessie Owens, Langston Hughes, and Ella Fitzgerald, to learn more about them and their achievements.

For a quick and easy way to assign names of the famous people to students, copy the activity cards on pages 118–119, cut them apart, and place them in a bag. (Create additional cards, if needed, to make sure there are enough for one per student.) Then have students take turns drawing a name from the bag. The name each student draws will be the subject of his or her research.

After students complete their research, have them record their findings on photocopies of the mini-book pages. To make the books, students should follow these directions:

1. Fold the two-sided page in half, so that the cover is on the outside.

2. Fill in the name of the famous person and draw his or her picture on the cover. Write your name on the author line.

3. Use your findings to fill in pages 2, 3, and 4.

4. If desired, add color and other embellishments, such as stickers and craft foam decorations, to personalize your book.

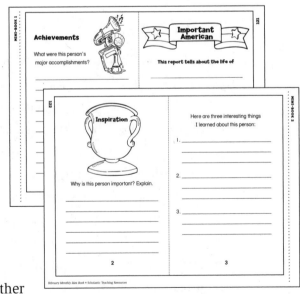

After students complete their mini-books, invite volunteers to share them with the class, as well as other information they'd like to share about what they learned from their research. Then, if desired, post the mini-books on a display similar to the one described in "Interactive Bulletin Board" on page 116.

INTERACTIVE BULLETIN BOARD

To prepare this engaging, hands-on display, make an enlarged photocopy of the activity board and cards on pages 117–119. Color and cut out the activity board and attach it to the center of a classroom bulletin board. Then cut apart the cards and display them randomly in the open spaces around the board. You can use the display in a number of ways to reinforce and enhance students' learning about famous African Americans. For example, you might do the following:

- Have students do the activity, as described in "The Contributions Activity" on page 114.

- Give clues about specific people named on the cards and challenge students to identify each person. Once the person is correctly named, ask a volunteer to name which category corresponds best to that person's contribution to our country.

- Invite small groups to remove the name cards, group the names by the contributions each person has made, then attach the grouped cards to the display to indicate the categories to which they belong.

- Sort and attach each name card to the corresponding category. Then display each student's "Important African American" mini-book near that person's name card.

READING LOG

Give each student photocopies of the reading logs on pages 123–124. (You might make double-sided copies of these pages.) Explain that students will select and read books that have been written by African Americans. In advance, you might want to gather a collection of these books—in a variety of genres—to place in your class library, or to work with the media specialist at your school to set up a section in the media center for this purpose. Encourage students to fill out a section on their reading logs for each book they read. After students complete their logs, invite them to tell about their favorite book on the log and to make recommendations to classmates about books they might want to read in the future.

Government

Literature

Entertainment

Music & Art

Where did I make my contribution?

Science/Technology

Civil Rights

Sports

Business

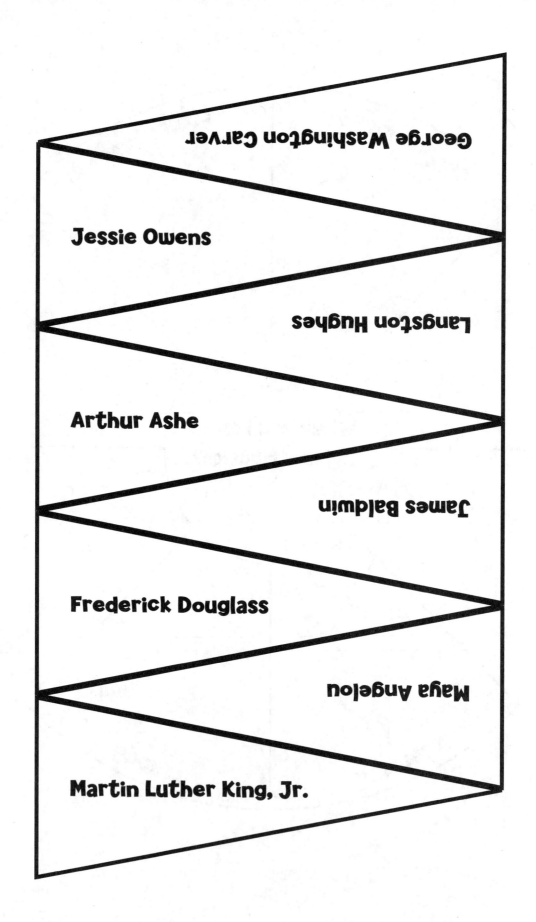

George Washington Carver

Jessie Owens

Langston Hughes

Arthur Ashe

James Baldwin

Frederick Douglass

Maya Angelou

Martin Luther King, Jr.

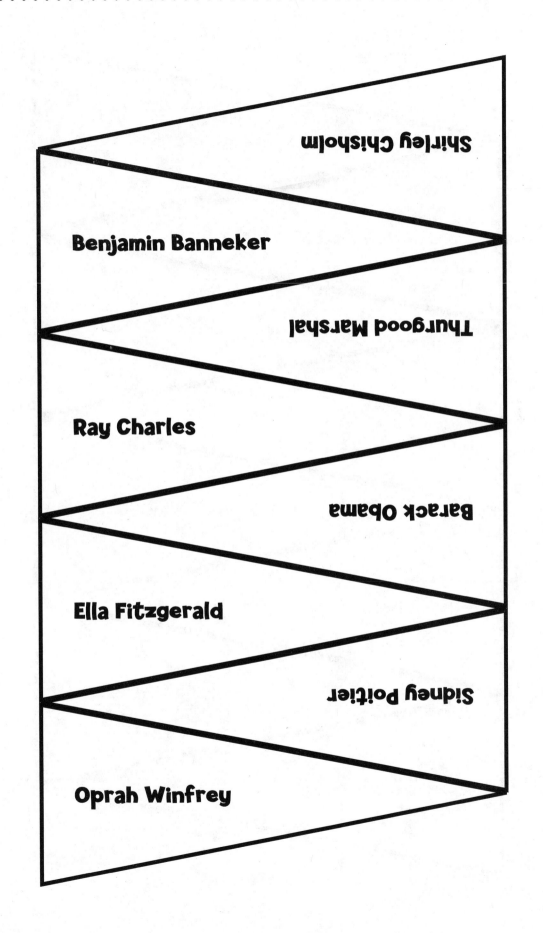

Shirley Chisholm

Benjamin Banneker

Thurgood Marshal

Ray Charles

Barack Obama

Ella Fitzgerald

Sidney Poitier

Oprah Winfrey

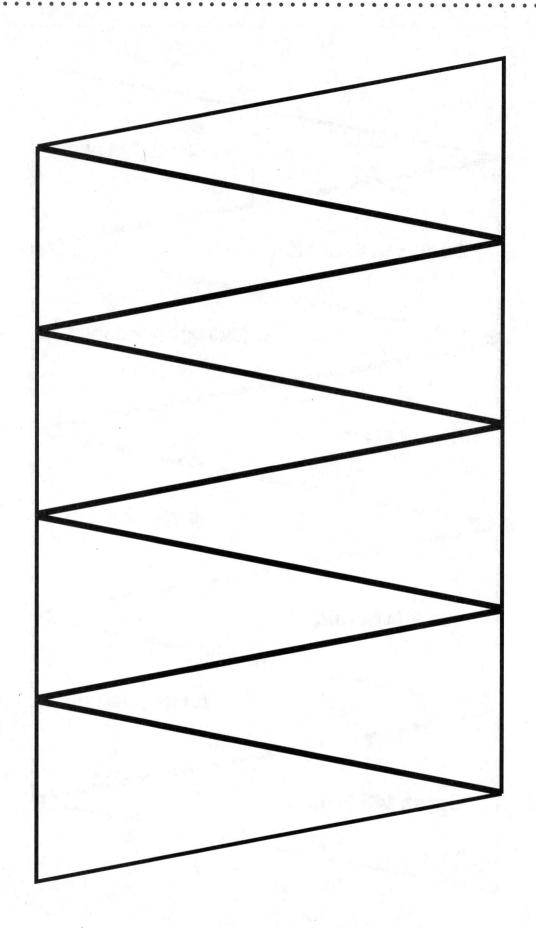

Achievements

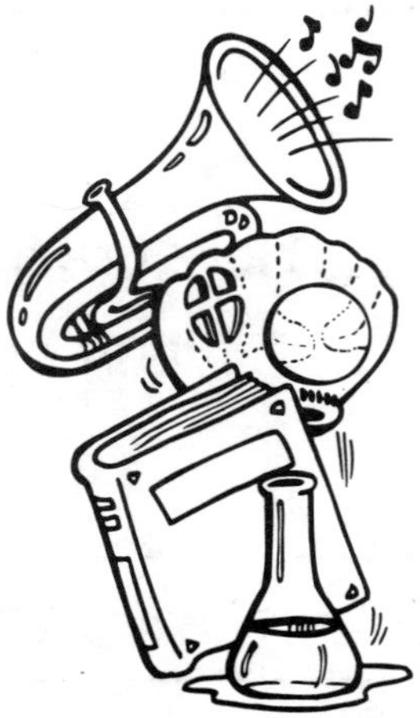

What were this person's major accomplishments?

4

Important American

This report tells about the life of

(Draw a picture of him or her.)

This report belongs to

(Name)

Here are three interesting things
I learned about this person:

1.

2.

3.

3

Inspiration

Why is this person important? Explain.

2

African-American Authors Reading Log

Record a list of books that you have read that were written by African American authors.

Title _____

Author _____

Illustrator _____

Would you recommend this book to a friend? Yes ❑   No ❑

Explain your reasons: _____

_____

_____

· ·

Title _____

Author _____

Illustrator _____

Would you recommend this book to a friend? Yes ❑   No ❑

Explain your reasons: _____

_____

_____

February Monthly Idea Book © Scholastic Teaching Resources

African-American Authors Reading Log

Record a list of books that you have read that were written by African American authors.

Title _____

Author _____

Illustrator _____

Would you recommend this book to a friend? Yes ❑   No ❑

Explain your reasons: _____

_____

_____

Title _____

Author _____

Illustrator _____

Would you recommend this book to a friend? Yes ❑   No ❑

Explain your reasons: _____

_____

_____

DENTAL HEALTH

February is Dental Health Month, providing you with a golden opportunity to instruct and encourage students to care for their teeth daily. As you discuss dental hygiene with students, explain that there are four different types of teeth, and each type does a different job. Then share the following:

Incisors—Located in the front of the mouth, these eight teeth have sharp, chisel-like crowns that are used to cut food.

Cuspids—There is one cuspid next to each lateral incisor. The pointed cuspids are used to help tear food.

Bicuspids—Four pairs of bicuspids are located next to the cuspids. These teeth are used to tear and crush food.

Molars—Three sets of molars are located on each side—top and bottom—of the back of the mouth. These large teeth are used to grind food. (As adults, most people need to have the 3rd set of molars, known as "wisdom teeth," surgically removed.)

Suggested Activities

★ ANATOMY OF A TOOTH

To familiarize students with the different parts of a tooth, distribute photocopies of the diagram on page 128. To begin, name and describe each part of the tooth (see below). You might point out each part on your own copy of the diagram. Then have students label their diagrams accordingly. (See the Answer Key, page 144, for the correct labels for the diagram.)

NAME _____ DATE _____

Parts-of-a-Tooth Diagram

Label the parts of this tooth with the correct words.

Crown   Dentin   Enamel   Pulp   Root

128

> **Crown:** The visible part of a tooth.
>
> **Enamel:** The hard, white outer covering of each tooth.
>
> **Root:** The part of the tooth that is anchored in the gum.
>
> **Dentin:** A bone-like tissue inside the tooth.
>
> **Pulp:** The soft center of each tooth that houses the nerves and blood vessels.

Tooth Decay Science

Demonstrate how acids eat away the enamel on teeth with this simple experiment. To begin, place an egg in a wide, clear glass filled with white vinegar. Show the glass to students and have them predict what will happen to the egg if you leave it in the vinegar for a period of time. Record their predictions on chart paper. Then set the glass aside where it can sit undisturbed overnight.

The next day, show the glass to students again. Invite them to share their observations about the egg and to compare the results with their predictions. Finally, explain that the vinegar caused the eggshell to soften, much in the same way that acid in foods and drinks can soften the enamel on a person's teeth. Go on to further explain that soft or weakened enamel provides less protection for teeth and can lead to cavities or tooth decay.

★ IMPRINTS AND INVENTORY

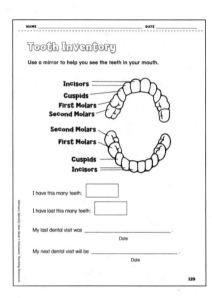

Students can make imprints of their teeth with this "cheesy" activity. Begin by giving each student an individually-wrapped slice of American cheese. Explain that after they peel the wrapper off, students will place the cheese slice between their teeth and gently bite down on it. Tell them that they should not bite through the cheese—they should apply just enough pressure to leave an impression of their teeth on the surface of the cheese slice. Also, tell them to carefully remove the cheese from their mouth after making their tooth impressions. Students can place their cheese slice on its original wrapper, or on a piece of waxed paper, so they can inspect their impressions.

As students examine the cheese impressions of their teeth, invite volunteers to share their observations about the shape and size of different teeth, how they are spaced, any missing teeth, and so on. Then, to take this activity a step further, distribute photocopies of page 129 to students. Ask them to take these "tooth inventories" home to complete. There, they can use a mirror to examine their teeth and have a family member help them count their teeth and fill out other information on the page. When students return their inventories to school, invite them to share their findings with the class. Afterward, you might share this information with students:

Most young children have 20 "baby" teeth, which eventually become loose, fall out, and are replaced by permanent teeth. Additional permanent teeth also grow in the back of the mouth. By the age of 13 or so, most children have grown a full set of permanent teeth—32 in all.

★ I LOST A TOOTH!

When a student loses a tooth at school, you can provide him or her with a special envelope in which to store the tooth and transport it safely home. To prepare, make several photocopies of the envelope pattern on page 130. Cut out each pattern, fold along the lines to form the envelope, and tuck the envelopes into your desk for safe keeping. Then, when a student loses a tooth, record his or her name and the date on the front of a lost-tooth envelope. Invite the student to color the envelope, then wrap his or her tooth in a tissue and place it in the envelope for the student to take home.

★ HEALTHY TEETH MINI-BOOK

Spark students' interest in caring for their teeth with this mini-book that they can complete and take home to share with family members. First, make two-sided copies of the mini-book pages. (Copy pages 131–132 back-to-back on one sheet of paper and pages 133–134 on another sheet.) Make a set of mini-book pages for each student. Then distribute the pages to students and have them do the following to complete their books:

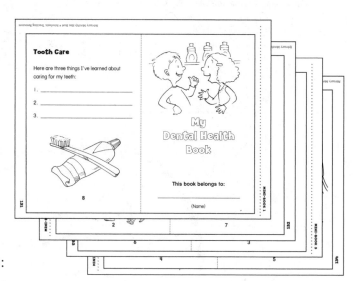

1. Fold each two-sided page in half.

2. Nest the pages together so that the cover is on top and the pages are properly sequenced. Staple the pages together along the left side.

3. Write your name on the author line on the cover.

4. Read each page and complete the activity, if applicable. On page 7, draw a picture of yourself flashing a big, toothy smile!

★ TOOTH FAIRY TALES

Talk with students about what it means to lose a tooth. Discuss some scientific reasons for how teeth become loose and fall out (or need to be pulled). Then invite volunteers to suggest some magical reasons for loosing their teeth. Afterward, explain that students will write their own creative stories about losing teeth. Distribute photocopies of the stationery on page 135 for students to use for their stories. Students might write an imaginary tale about how they would handle pulling a loose tooth and what they would do with the tooth once it has been pulled. Students could also write about how they would prepare for a visit from the "Tooth Fairy," what the Tooth Fairy does with all the teeth she collects, or how she manages

to move around in the night without detection. Or, students might create an entirely new character that has magical qualities that are revealed to children who have a loose tooth or have lost a tooth. Invite students to share their completed stories with the class.

Parts-of-a-Tooth Diagram

Label the parts of this tooth with the correct words.

Crown   Dentin   Enamel   Pulp   Root

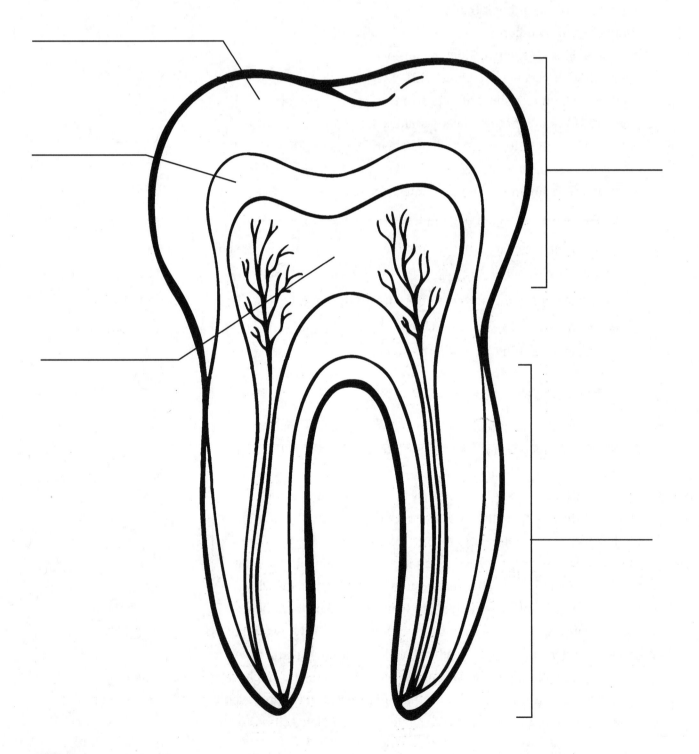

February Monthly Idea Book © Scholastic Teaching Resources

Tooth Inventory

Use a mirror to help you see the teeth in your mouth.

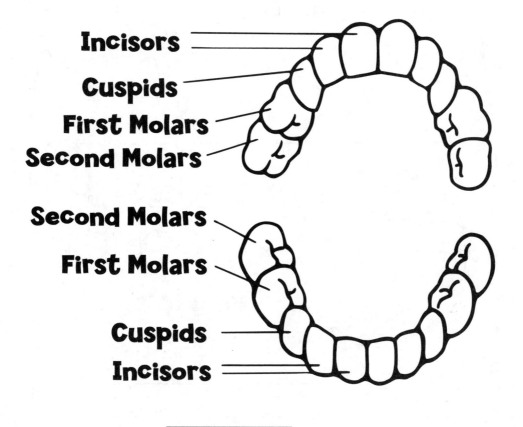

Incisors

Cuspids

First Molars

Second Molars

Second Molars

First Molars

Cuspids

Incisors

I have this many teeth: ☐

I have lost this many teeth: ☐

My last dental visit was _____ .

Date

My next dental visit will be _____ .

Date

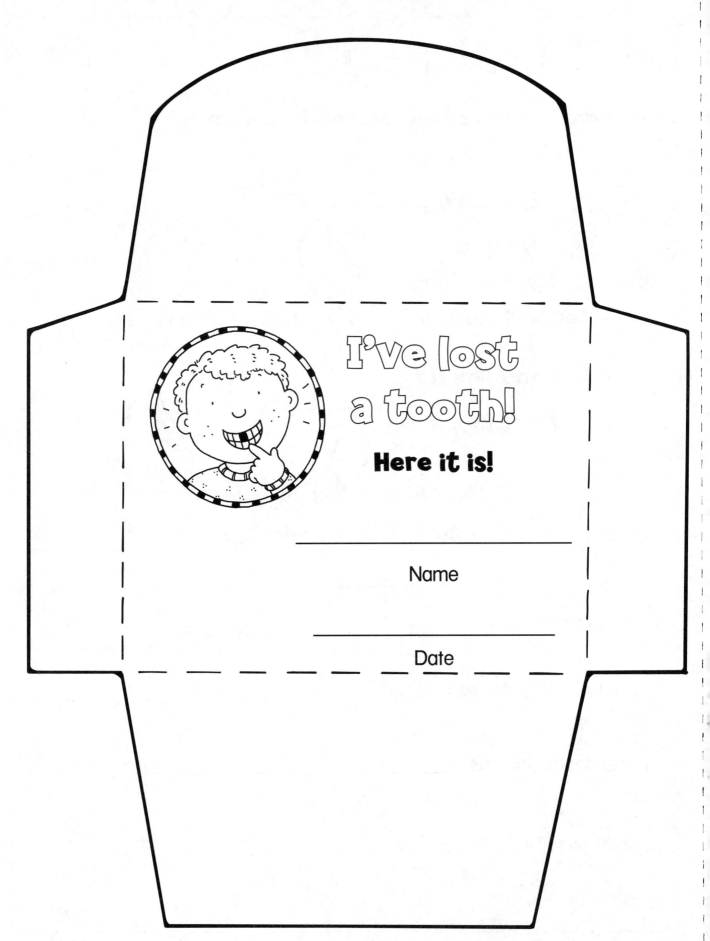

I've lost a tooth!

Here it is!

_____

Name

_____

Date

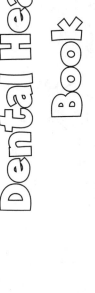

My
Dental Health
Book

This book belongs to:

_____

(Name)

Tooth Care

Here are three things I've learned about caring for my teeth:

1. _____

2. _____

3. _____

8

My Supplies

What supplies do you need to keep your teeth and gums healthy? Check the box beside each item on the list.

☐ toothbrush

☐ toothpaste

☐ dental floss

☐ fluoride rinse

2

Here is how my smile looks:

7

Learn How to Floss!

To get started, tear a piece of dental floss about the length of your arm.

1. Hold the floss between your thumbs and forefingers, as shown.

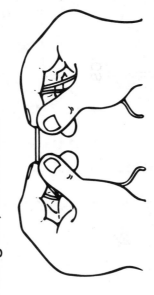

2. Work the floss between your teeth. Gently move it up and down.

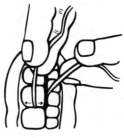

3. Floss between all of your teeth, including your molars.

3

Healthy Habits

Will each of these habits help keep your teeth healthy?

Write Y for yes. Write N for no.

____ Brush your teeth once a week.

____ Visit a dentist if your tooth hurts.

____ Drink sugary drinks and soda daily.

____ Floss between your teeth every day.

____ Visit a dentist twice a year.

6

Word Find Fun

```
T O O T H P A S T E
C B C E E F G R F D
R X T N X X Q O I E
O B C A E C R O L N
W S U M B A X T L T
N P N E R V E H I I
D U X L U I X Z N N
F L O S S T G H G J
X P N X H Y B W Q X
```

Find and circle these words in the puzzle above:

BRUSH	CAVITY	CROWN	DENTIN
ENAMEL	FILLING	FLOSS	NERVE
PULP	ROOT	TOOTHPASTE

4

Learn How to Brush!

1. Brush your teeth at an angle. Set the bristles of the toothbrush toward your gums.

2. Gently massage your gums and roll the brush toward the edge of each tooth.

3. Make sure the bristles go between your teeth.

4. Brush the back of each tooth.

5

AWARDS, INCENTIVES, AND MORE

Getting Started

Make several photocopies of the reproducibles on pages 138 through 142. Giving out the bookmarks, pencil toppers, notes, and certificates will show students your enthusiasm for their efforts and achievements. Plus, bookmarks and pencil toppers are a fun treat for students celebrating birthdays.

- Provide materials for decorating, including markers, color pencils, and stickers.

- Encourage students to bring home their creations to share and celebrate with family members.

★ BOOKMARKS

1. Photocopy onto tagboard and cut apart.

2. For more fanfare, punch a hole in one end and tie on a length of colorful ribbon or yarn.

★ PENCIL TOPPERS

1. Photocopy onto tagboard and cut out.

2. Use an art knife to cut through the Xs.

3. Slide a pencil through the Xs as shown.

SEND-HOME NOTES

1. Photocopy and cut apart.

2. Record the child's name and the date.

3. Add your signature.

4. Add more details about the student's day on the back of the note.

CERTIFICATES

1. Photocopy.

2. Record the child's name and other information, as directed.

3. Add details about the child's achievement (if applicable), then add your signature and the date.

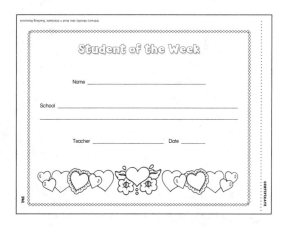

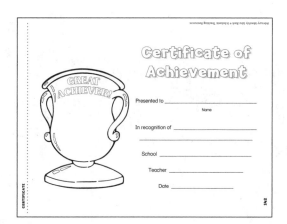

Mr. Groundhog

WAKE UP! VISIT THE LIBRARY!

Zzzzz

Be a Reader!

I love to Read.

_____
Student's Name

was a "sweetheart" in class today!

_____
Date

_____
Teacher

_____
Student's Name

earned my praise today!

For:

_____
_____
_____

_____   _____
Date   Teacher

_____
Student's Name

was extra good today!

_____   _____
Date   Teacher

I was all smiles because . . .

_____
_____
_____
_____

_____   _____
Date   Teacher

February Monthly Idea Book © 2012, Scholastic Teaching Resource

Student of the Week

Name

School

Teacher

Date

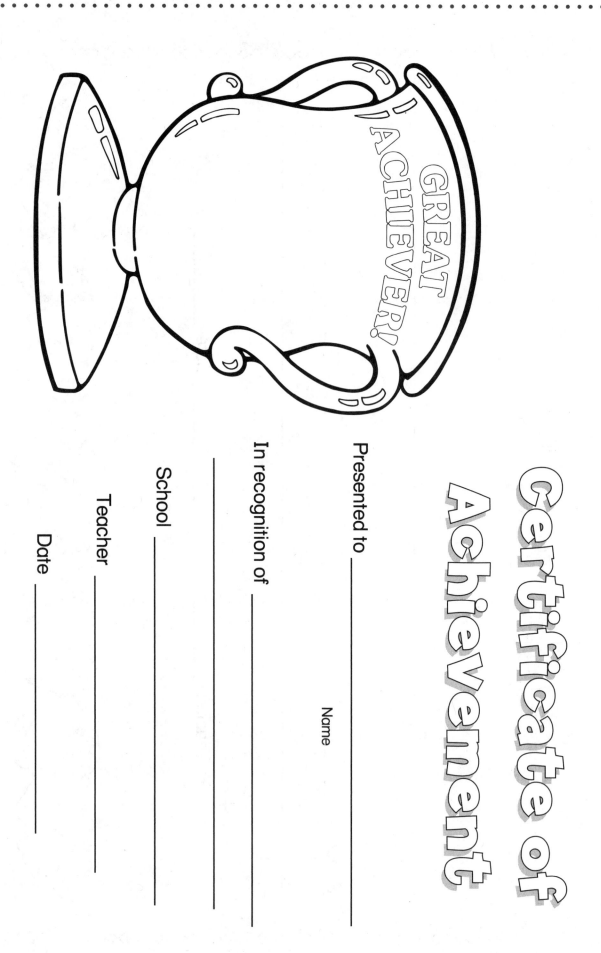

GREAT ACHIEVER!

Certificate of Achievement

Presented to

_____

Name

In recognition of

_____

School

_____

Teacher

_____

Date

_____

Groundhog Day Word Find, page 37

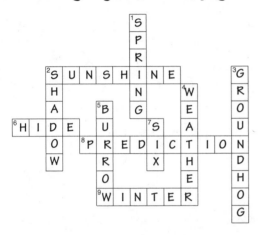

Groundhog Day Crossword, page 38

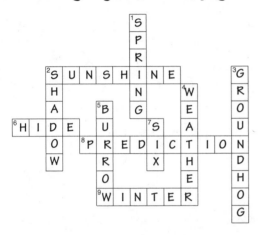

Undergroundhog Burrow Maze, page 39

Valentine's Day Crossword, page 48

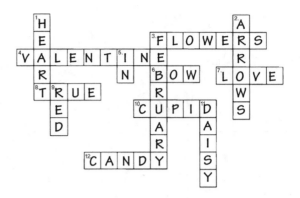

Parts-of-a-Heart Diagram, page 68

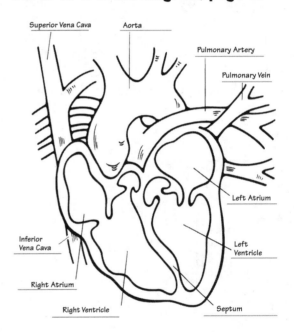

Superior Vena Cava
Aorta
Pulmonary Artery
Pulmonary Vein
Left Atrium
Inferior Vena Cava
Left Ventricle
Right Atrium
Right Ventricle
Septum

Presidents' Day Word Find, page 84

Parts-of-a-Tooth Diagram, page 128

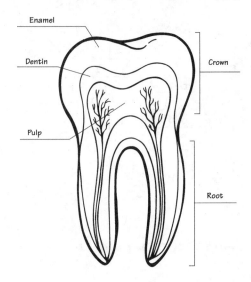

"My Dental Health Book" Mini-Book, page 134

Page 4:

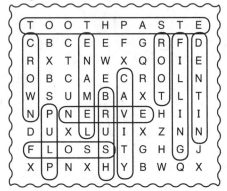

Page 6:

N_____ Brush your teeth once a week.

Y_____ Visit a dentist if your tooth hurts.

N_____ Drink sugary drinks and soda daily.

Y_____ Floss between your teeth every day.

Y_____ Visit a dentist twice a year.